LINE DESIGNS

Grades 5 and up

By
Dale Seymour, Linda Silvey and Joyce Snider

Published by Ideal School Supply
an imprint of

Authors: Dale Seymour, Linda Silvey, Joyce Snider

 Children's Publishing

Published by Ideal School Supply
An imprint of McGraw-Hill Children's Publishing
Copyright © 1974 McGraw-Hill Children's Publishing

All Rights Reserved • Printed in the United States of America

Limited Reproduction Permission: Permission to duplicate these materials is limited to the person for whom they are purchased. Reproduction for an entire school or school district is unlawful and strictly prohibited.

Send all inquiries to:
McGraw-Hill Children's Publishing
3195 Wilson Drive NW
Grand Rapids, Michigan 49544

Line Designs—grades 5 and up
ISBN: 1-56451-081-6

2 3 4 5 6 7 8 9 PHXBK 08 07 06 05 04 03

CONTENTS

INTRODUCTION	5
BASIC INSTRUCTIONS	7
BEGINNING WORK SHEETS	10
SPECIAL EFFECTS	16
CREATING YOUR OWN DESIGNS	18
THE LINE-DIVIDER™	20
POLYGONAL DESIGNS AND WORKSHEETS	22
LINE DESIGNS IN CIRCLES	42
LINE DESIGN SPIRALS	44
COMPLEX LINE DESIGNS	46
ALPHABET DESIGNS	52
HOLIDAY DESIGNS AND WORKSHEETS	55
LINE DESIGN MOSAICS	60
CURVE STITCHING	72
GEOMETRIC CONSTRUCTIONS	76

INTRODUCTION

We have consistently found that a unit on geometric constructions or line designs has been the most motivating and absorbing topics in our classrooms. Creating geometric designs allows students an opportunity to exercise creativity and imagination. The students discover a surprising number of geometric relationships as they develop a new appreciation for the beauty of geometry.

Students will learn more mathematics from a unit on line designs if it is preceded by a unit on geometric constructions. Teachers generally agree that making line designs is popular with students, however, they often relate that they feel guilty, that this is not teaching students mathematics.

For some reason, many teachers think that math education in the early school years should consist of nothing but computation. This is precisely why students begin to dislike math in many cases. Students need a variety of mathematical activities. They need to see that mathematics, like other disciplines, can be beautiful; that mathematics underlies much of the design and art of our modern culture. Designing a geometric thread sculpture is one way for your students to begin to experience the beauty of mathematics and to understand its relevance.

Students enjoy expressing their creativity in their designs. Displaying student work will illustrate the value of neatness, accuracy and knowledge of geometric fundamentals.

One of the best features of an enrichment unit on geometric constructions and line designs is its appeal to students with a wide range of abilities. Reluctant learners are usually as interested as high achievers. Since few prerequisite skills are needed, some students who have frequently failed in previous mathematical tasks, experience success and peer approval for the first time.

We hope you and your students enjoy creating line designs as much as we have.

Dale Seymour
Linda Silvey
Joyce Snider

BASIC INSTRUCTIONS

WHAT ARE LINE DESIGNS?

Line designs are geometric patterns formed entirely by the use of straight line segments that produce the illusion of a curve. When first seeing one of these designs you will have to look closely to convince yourself that no curved lines are used. This interesting property produces fascinating results yet line designs are relatively simple to do.

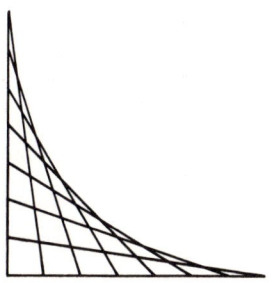 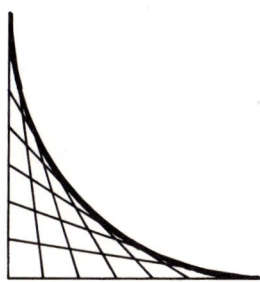

HOW ARE THEY MADE?

These line designs are formed by connecting certain sequences of points with line segments Different designs are formed by selecting points in various ways. The most common way is to connect equally-spaced points along the two sides of an angle as shown and described below.

(1) Draw an angle with two sides of the same length.
(2) Divide each side into an equal number of segments and mark them as shown in figure 1.
(3) Connect point A with point A, point B with point B, and so on as shown in figure 2 until all of the points are connected.

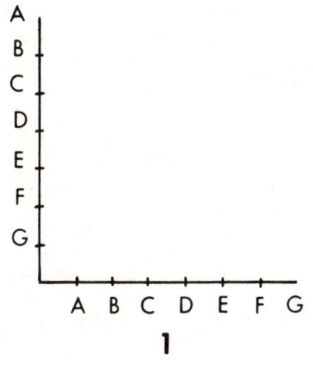 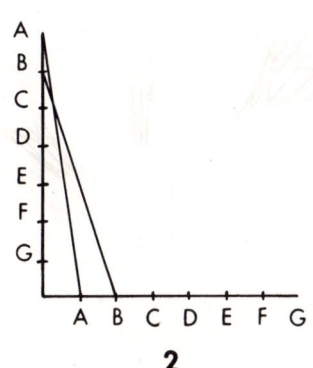 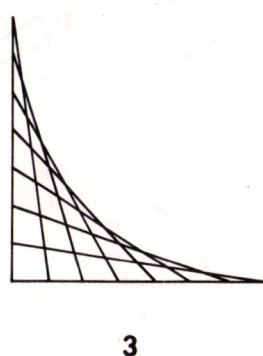

      1   2   3

Line Designs   ©Ideal School Supply Company

DESIGN EFFECTS AND VARIATIONS

A greater number of divisions on the side of an angle will result in a design which is more dense. After some practice you will be able to determine the number of divisions necessary to give you the design result that pleases you.

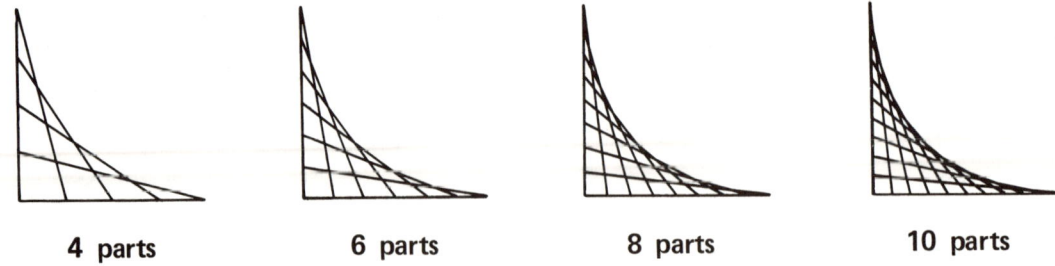

4 parts   6 parts   8 parts   10 parts

The angle which is the basis for your design may be any size you wish. A variety of angle sizes are shown below.

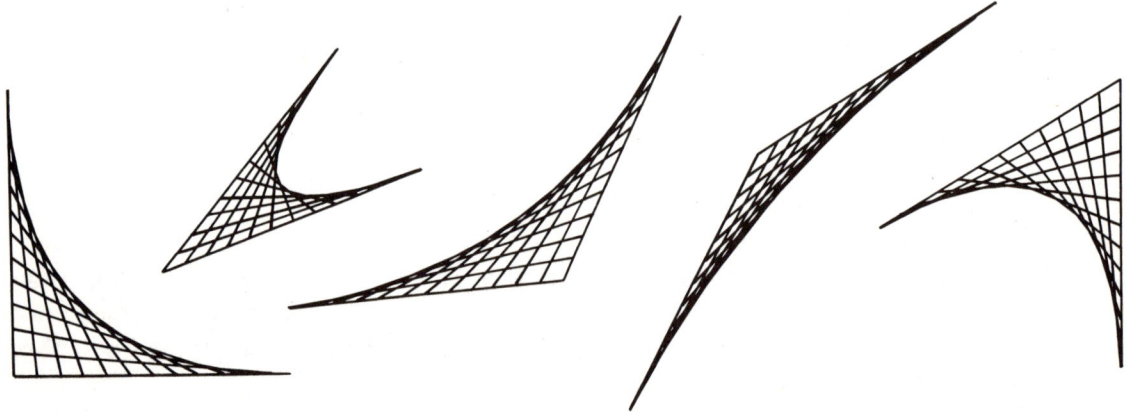

The sides of the angle need not be the same length. However, divide each side into the same number of equal parts.

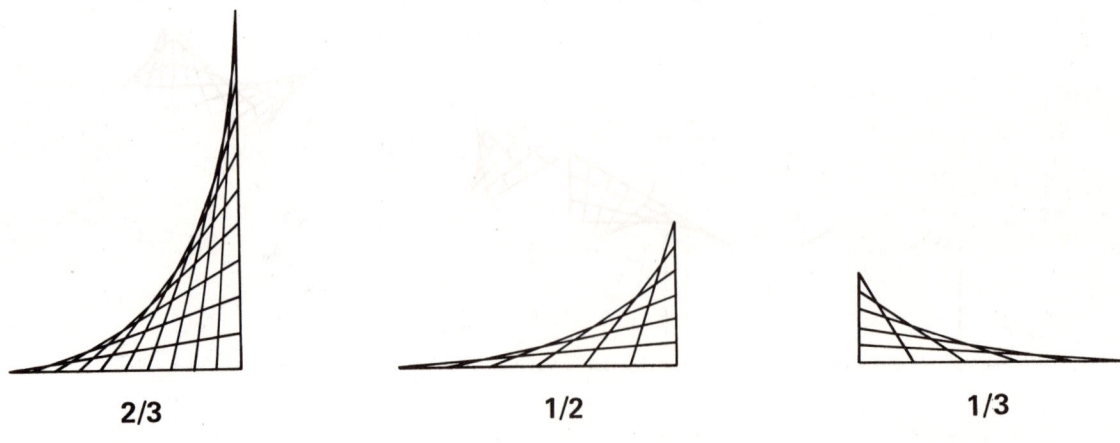

2/3   1/2   1/3

MAKING DESIGNS BY COMBINING ANGLES

By combining two or more angles a variety of designs can be produced. Complete each angle using the basic line design technique.

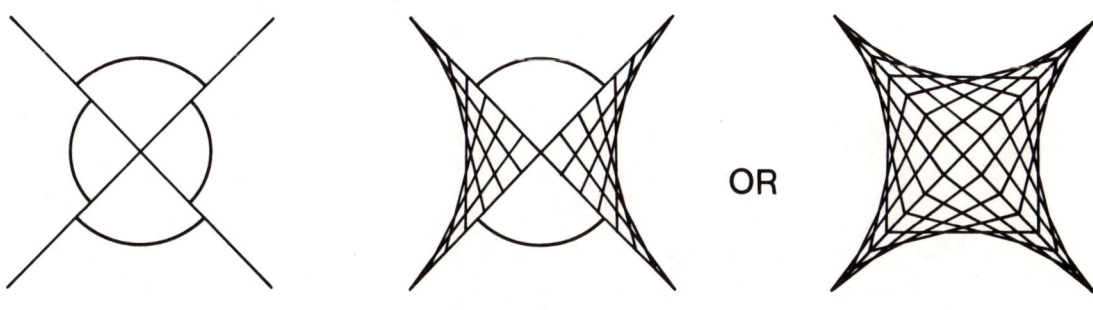

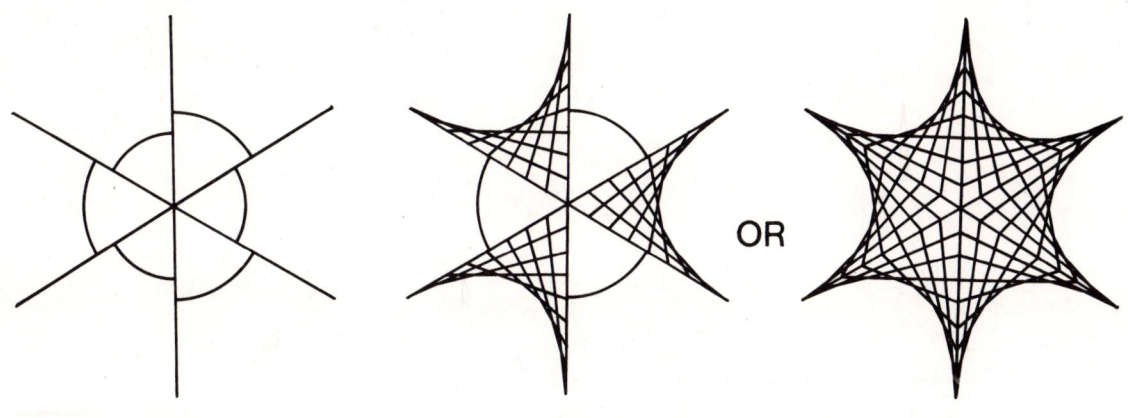

Line Designs

LINE DESIGNS WORKSHEET ONE

This worksheet will show you how to make beautiful geometric curves, called line designs, by drawing a series of straight line segments.

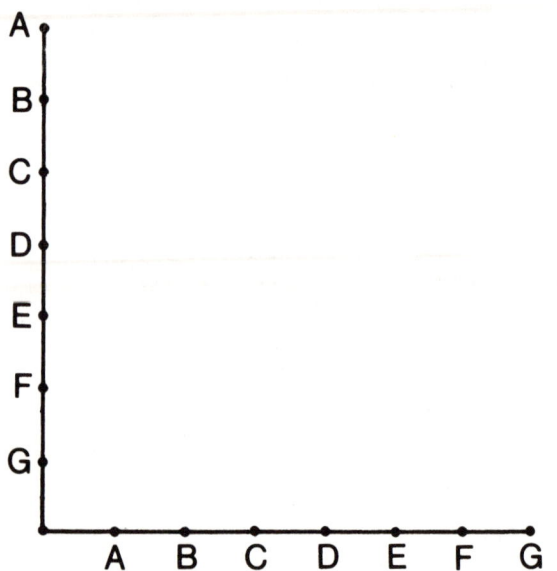

1. In the figure above connect like letters (A to A, B to B, etc.) with a straight edge.

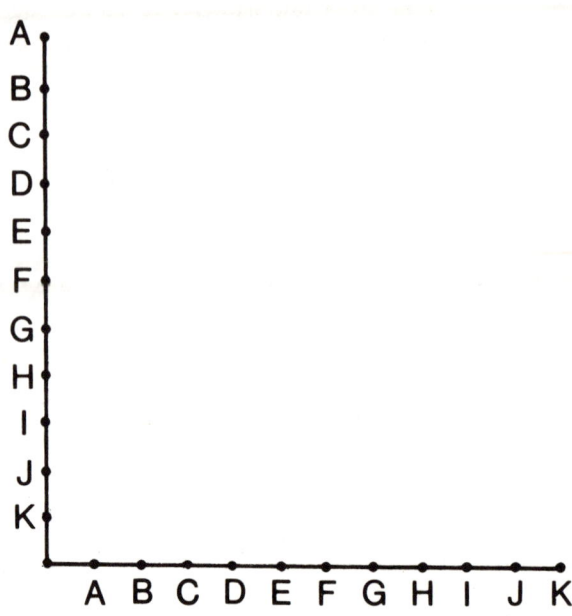

2. Notice the "Curve" that was formed by the series of straight segments. The two sides of the angle are divided into an equal number of equal parts. Connect the like letters above and notice the difference in the design when the equal parts are closer together.

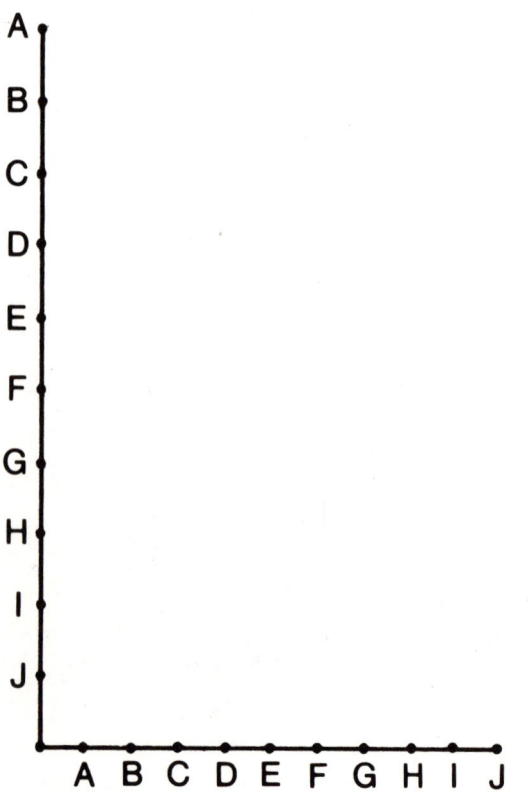

3. The two sides of the angle do not need to be equal in length. However, they do need to be divided into the same number of parts. Connect the like letters above to see the effect.

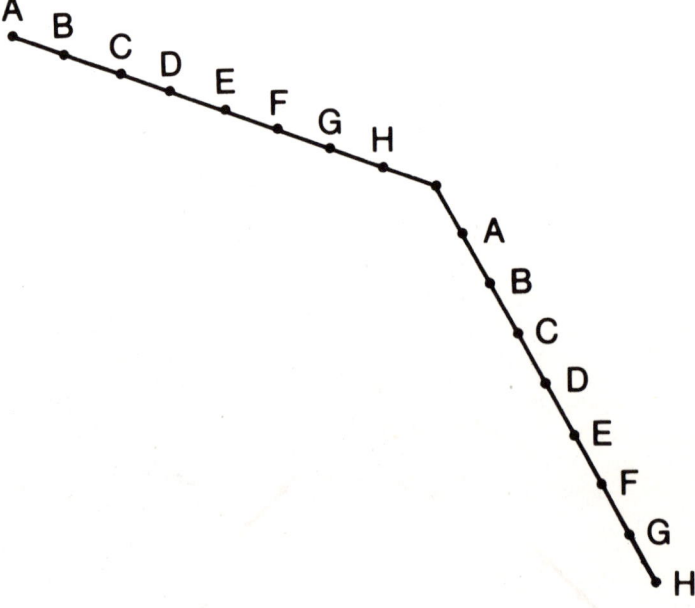

4. The angle which is the basis for the line design need not be a right angle. Connect the like letters of the obtuse angle above to see the effect.

Line Designs   ©Ideal School Supply Company

LINE DESIGNS WORKSHEET TWO

The most common type of line design is one that is formed by several angles. Use the technique you learned with worksheet one to complete the designs below.

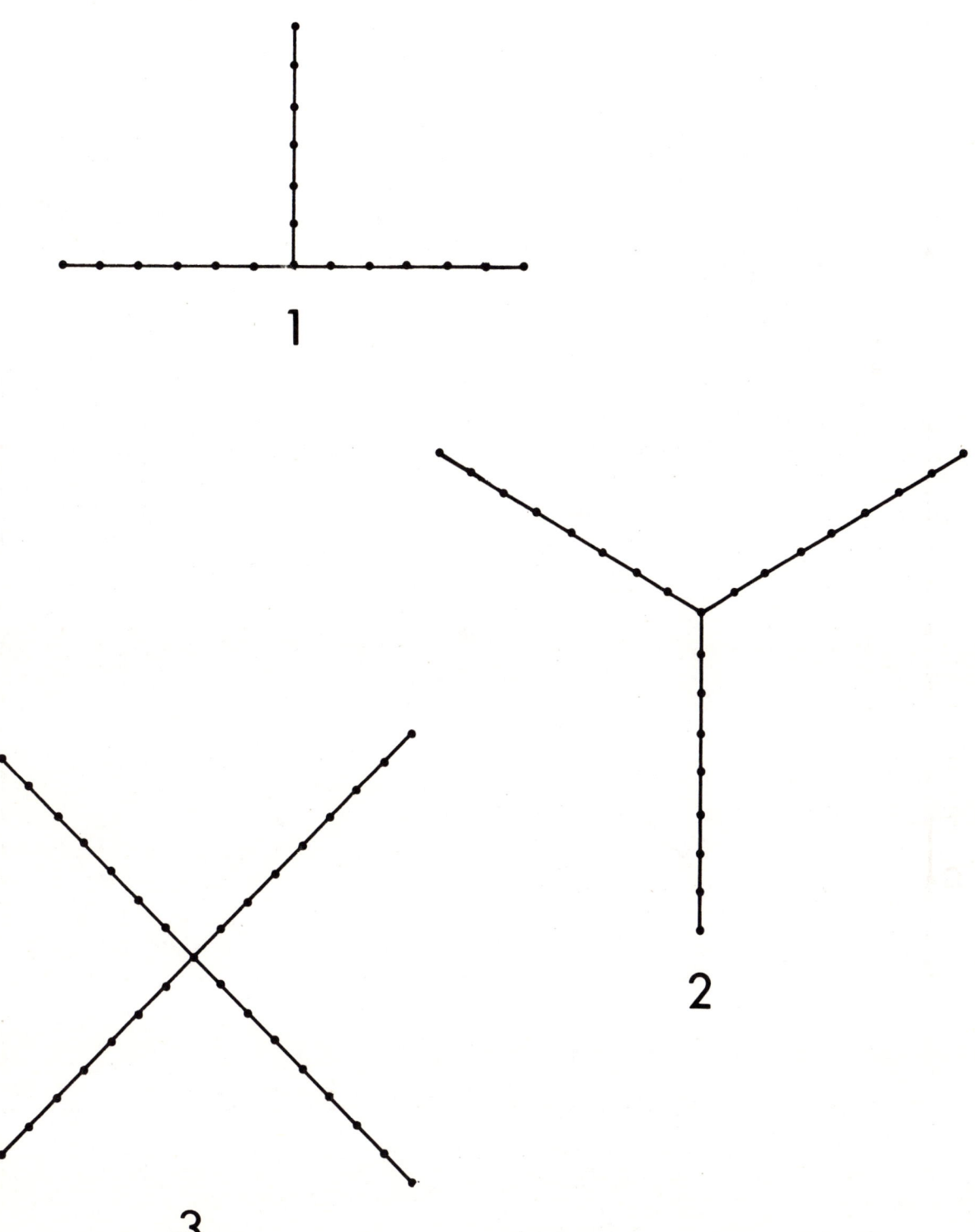

Line Designs

LINE DESIGNS WORKSHEET THREE

The square below can be thought of as eight angles.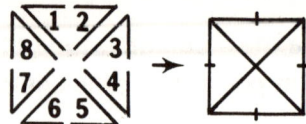

"Fill-in" the eight angles below to form a line design. Your final result should look similar to the design on page 34.

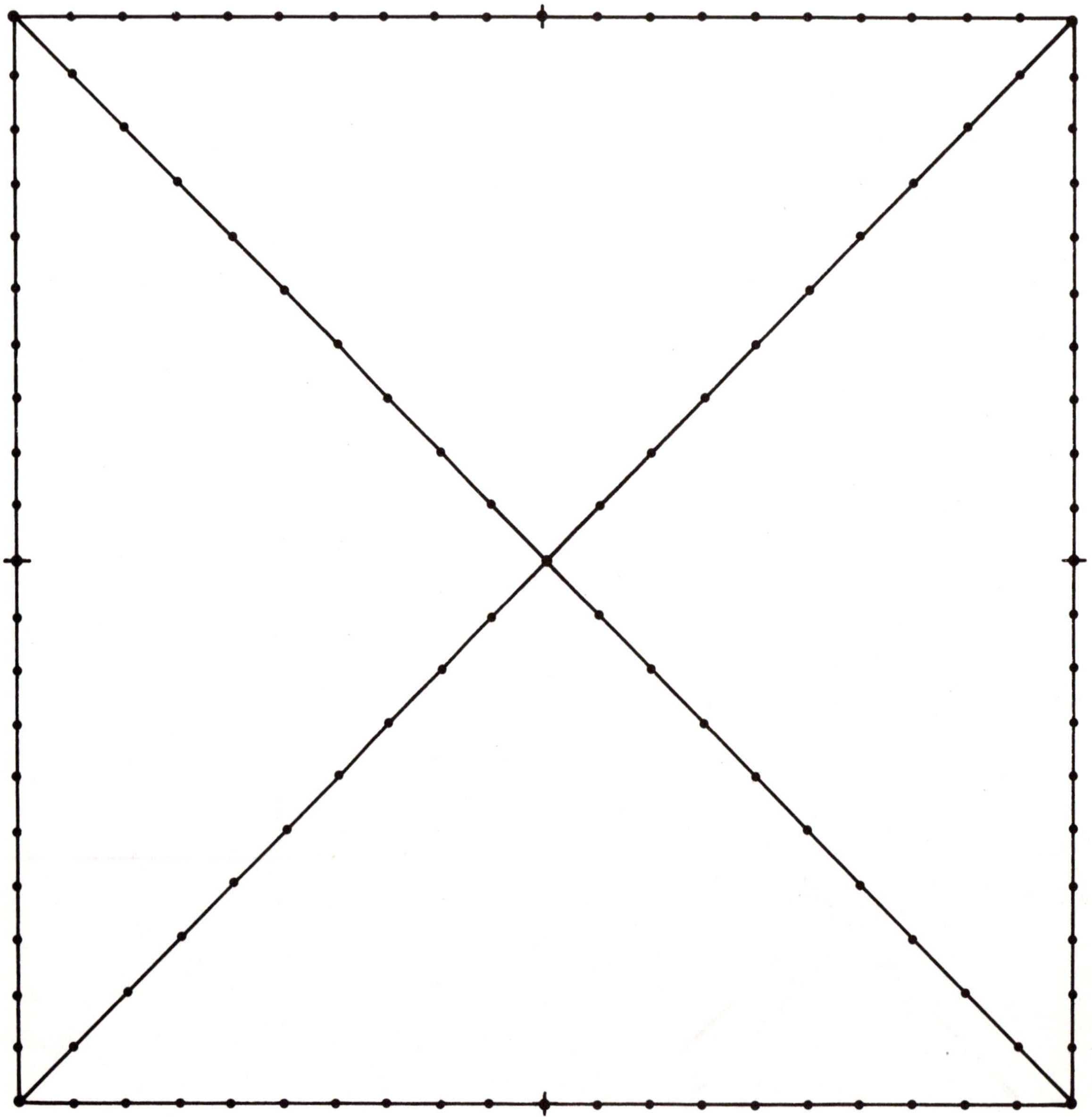

LINE DESIGNS WORKSHEET FOUR

Divide the two sides of each angle below into an equal number of equal parts. Connect the division points using the line design technique.

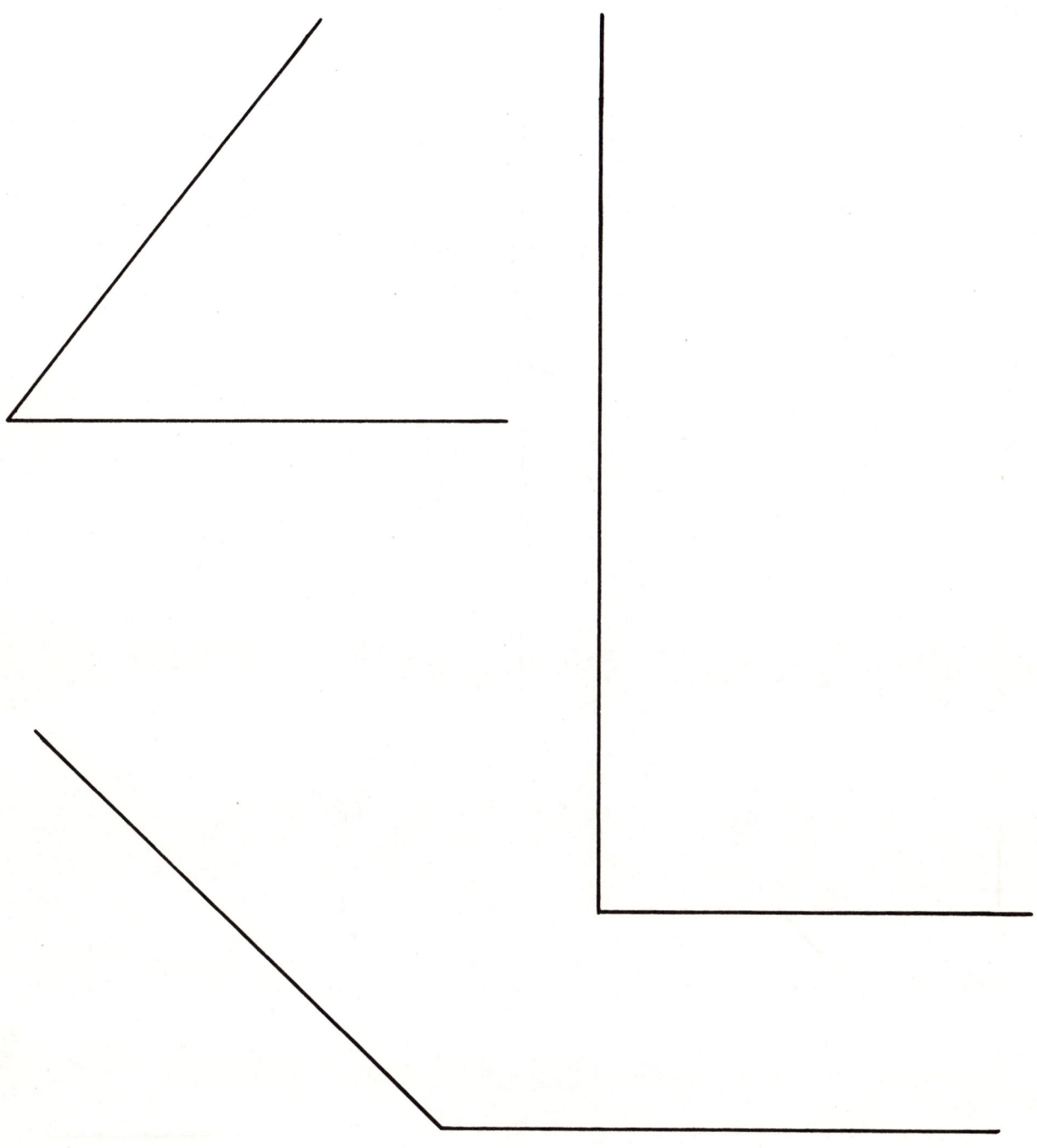

Line Designs 13 ©Ideal School Supply Company

LINE DESIGN WORKSHEET FIVE

Divide the three line segments below into an equal number of equal parts. "Fill-in" the three angles using the line design technique.

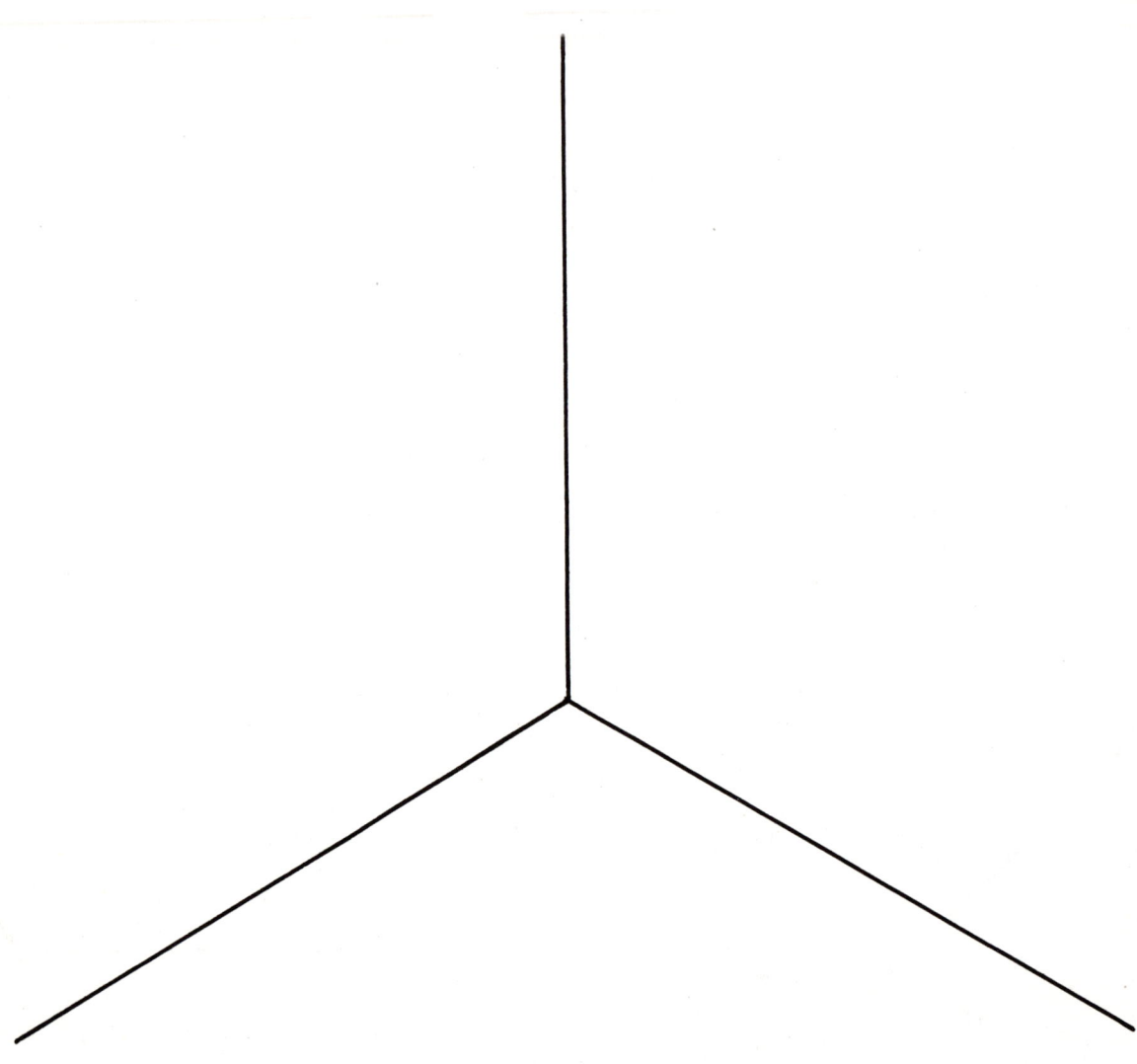

Line Designs

LINE DESIGN WORKSHEET SIX

The circle below is divided into twenty-four equal arcs. Connect each point with every one of the other 23 points by a line segment. Be accurate and you will be pleased with the resulting design.

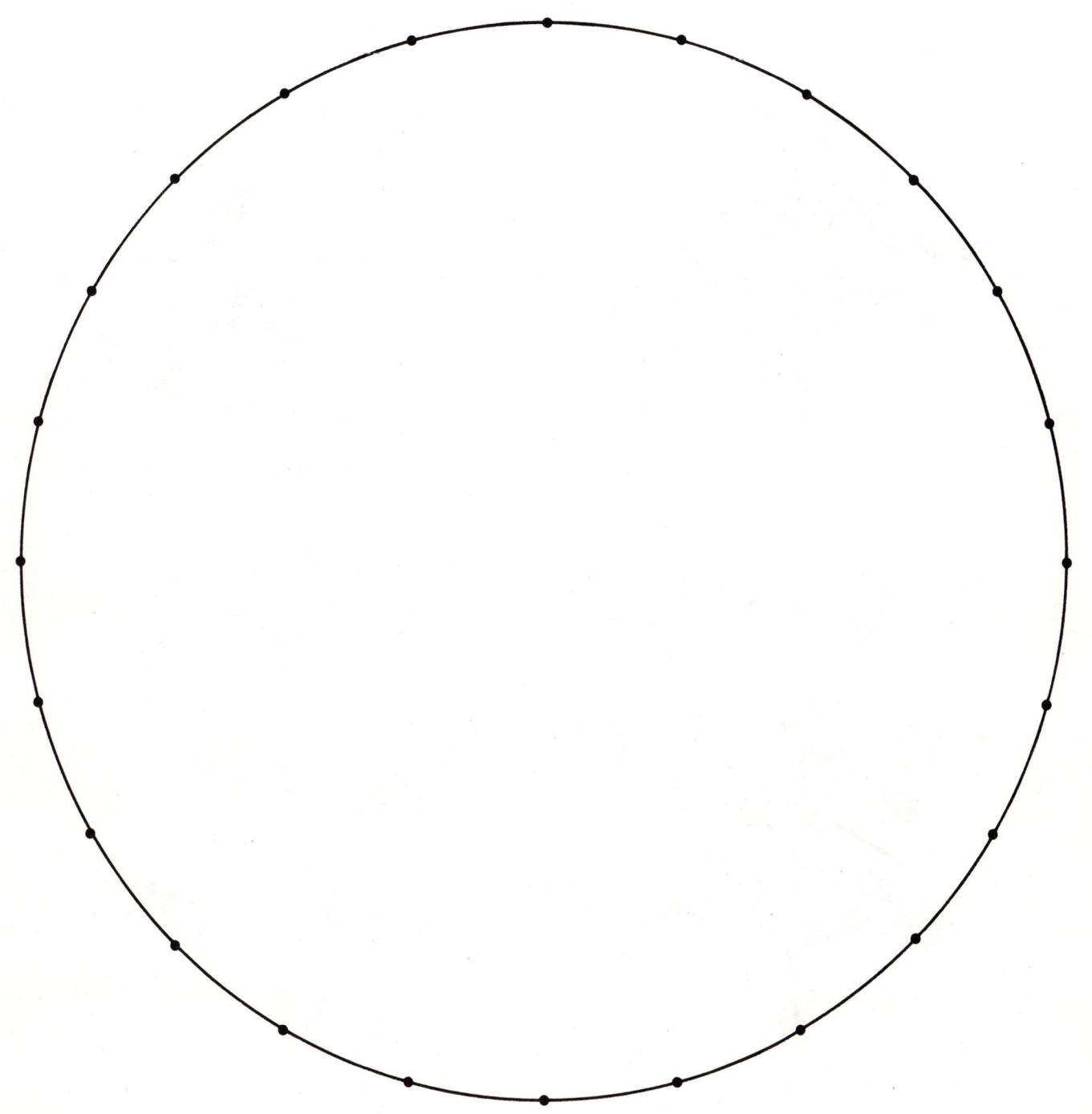

Line Designs

DESIGN EFFECTS FROM SHADING

The four line designs shown below have taken on new design features because they have been shaded. Colored pencils, felt tip pens, or other materials can help make your designs more attractive.

Line Designs

DESIGN EFFECTS FROM OVERLAPPING

An interesting illusion of depth can be accomplished by overlapping one design, or a part of a design, over another. The four designs below are examples of overlapping. One approach is to draw one complete design over the other as is done in the pentagon on the lower left of the page. The other method is to draw a line which stops at the point where it appears to pass under another part of the design. When you are drawing the lines which disappear beneath other lines, it is very important to line up the proper endpoints each time. Overlapping is not for beginners.

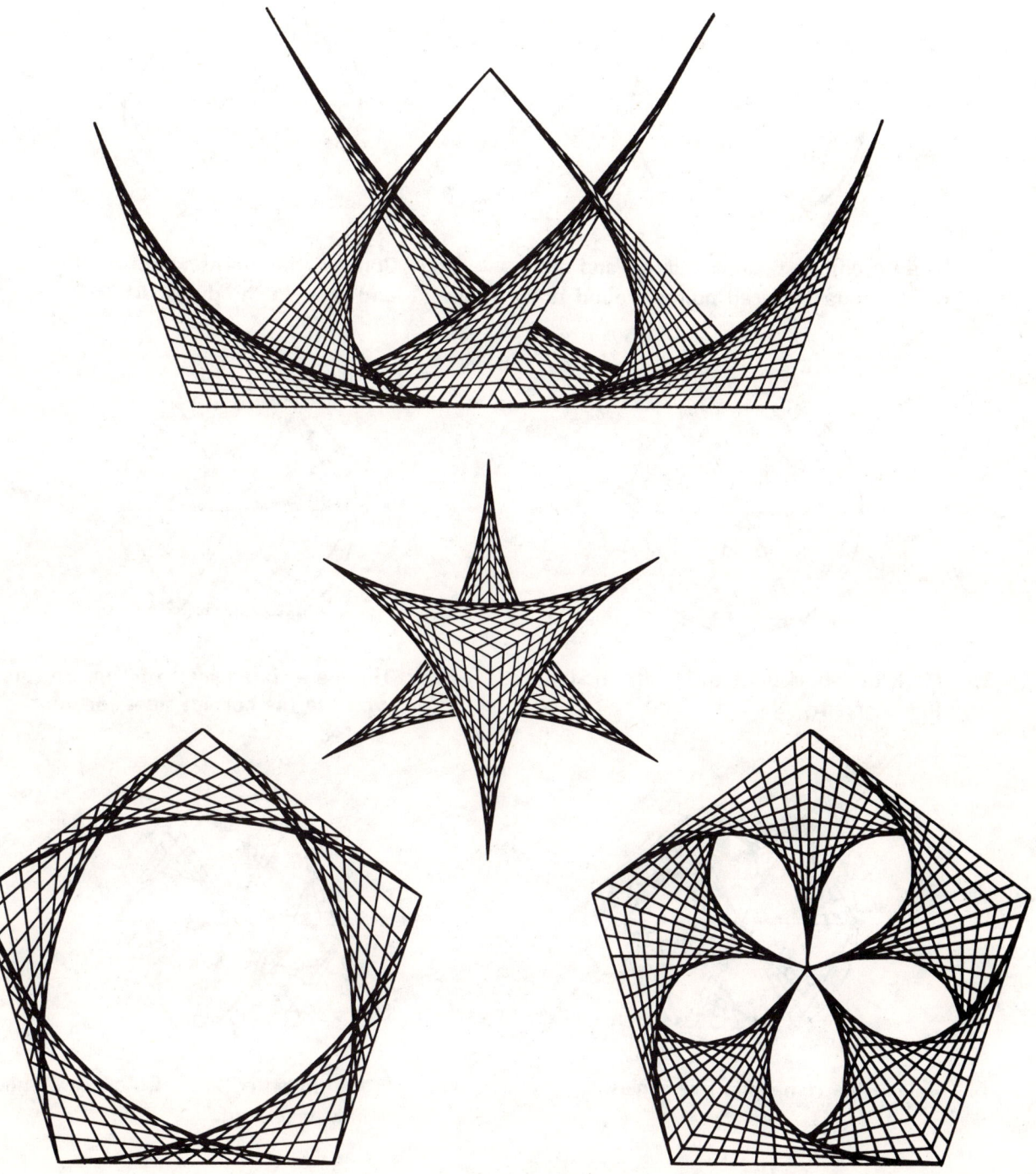

Line Designs

17

©Ideal School Supply Company

CREATING YOUR OWN DESIGNS

After you have learned how to make some of the simpler designs, you will probably want to try some of the more complicated ones shown in this book. Choose a design and analyze it carefully. Is it based on a geometric figure? What line segments do you need to draw to form the sides of the angles? Shown here are the steps you can take to create a typical design.

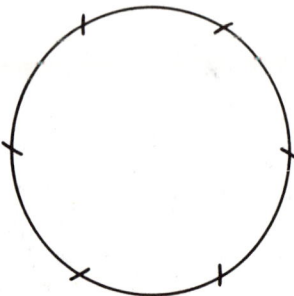

1. Using a compass, draw a circle and mark off six equally-spaced points around it.

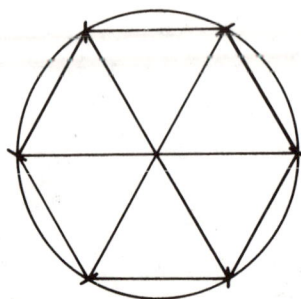

2. Connect the points to form a hexagon and draw in the diagonals shown.

3. Mark off equal units of length on all line segments.

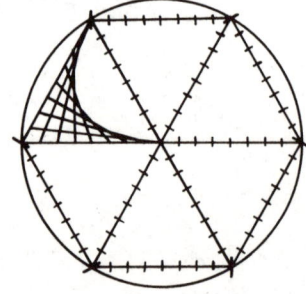

4. There are six angles to fill in. Be sure you use the correct sides for your angles.

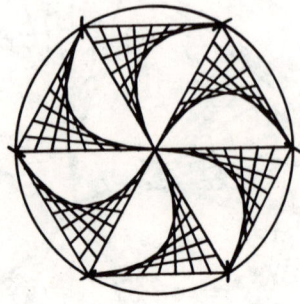

5. Fill in the remaining five angles.

6. Erase unwanted lines. Color, sew, shade, or ink as desired.

Line Designs

18

©Ideal School Supply Company

CREATING DESIGNS FROM GEOMETRIC FIGURES

Many beautiful designs can be made from regular polygons. With simple geometric constructions you can locate points for these designs. The following are some examples made from angles formed by such figures. The designs on pages 22 to 41 of this book are based on regular polygons.

If you are not familiar with basic geometric constructions, you may wish to refer to pages 76 to 78 in this book. The companion book to *Line Designs, Creative Constructions*, provides instruction and examples that will enable you to create a wide variety of basic designs for line design.

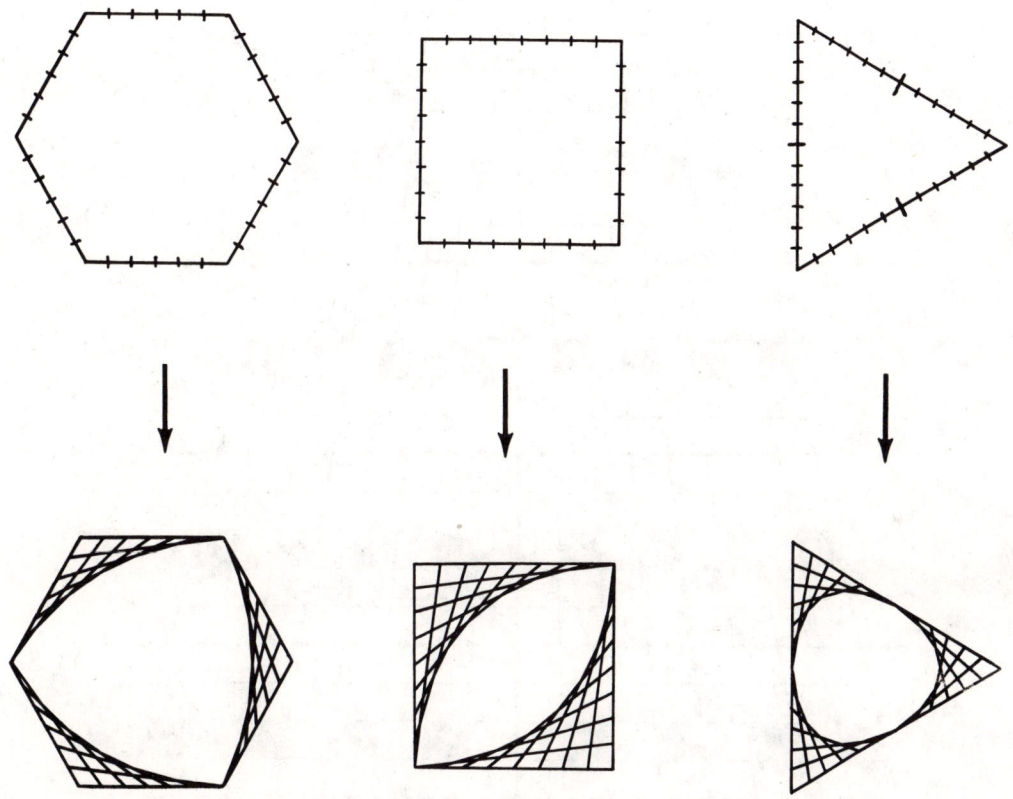

THE LINE-DIVIDER™

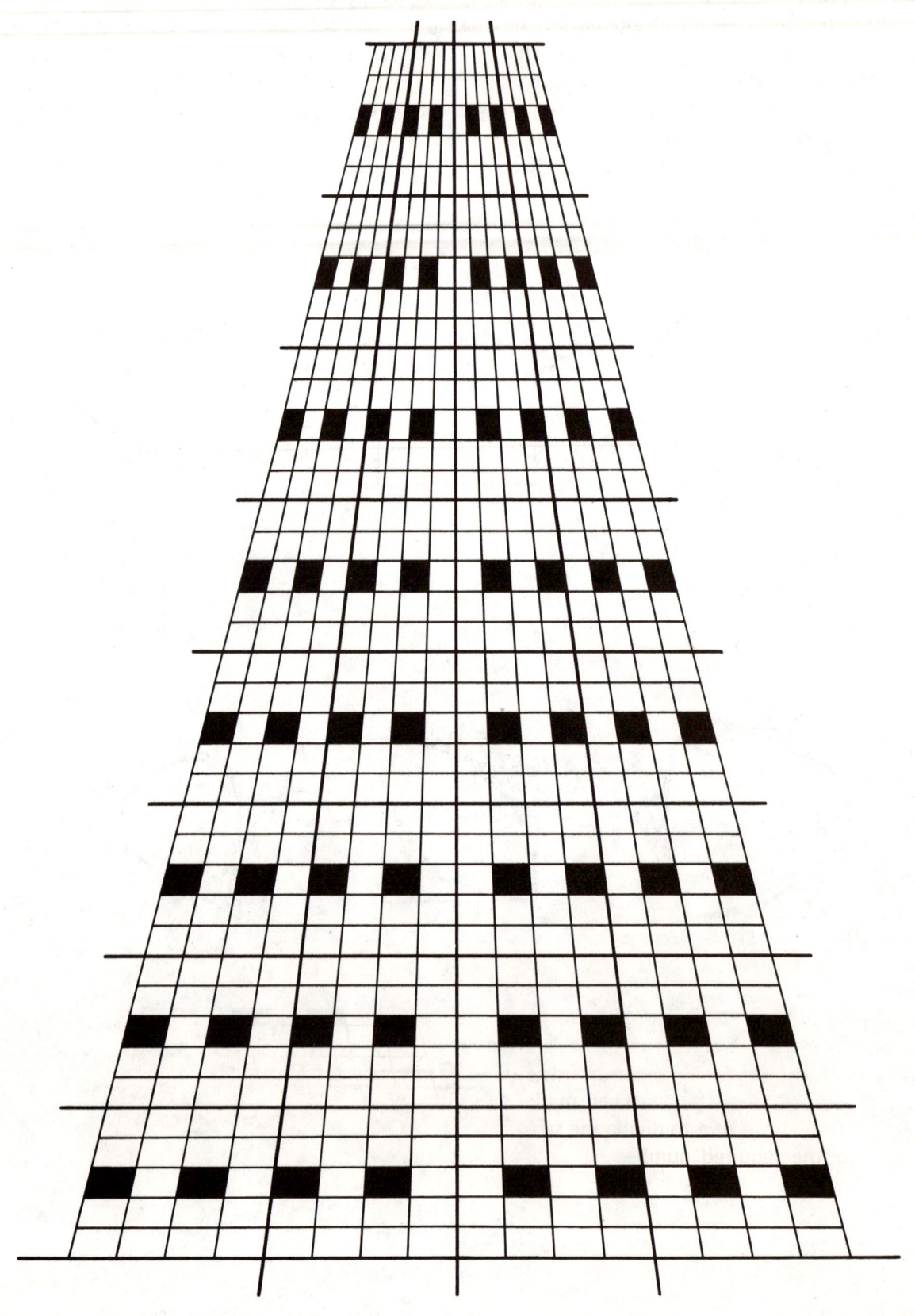

Line Designs

USING THE LINE-DIVIDER™

The Line-Divider™ on the preceding page will enable you to divide a line segment into sixteen or fewer equal parts quickly and easily. It was used to divide the lines in many designs in this book. This tool was created to ensure accuracy and save time and effort.

If you are making your line design on transparent material or tracing paper, place the sheet over the Line-Divider™ page, a reproduction of the page, or a transparent copy of the page. Trace the division marks onto the segments in your design. Hold both pages against a window or place on a light table if necessary.

If you are making a line design on an opaque surface, mark the length of your segment on the edge of a card. Then lay the card on top of the Line-Divider™ page, or a copy of it, and mark the divisions on the edge of the card. Transfer the division marks from the card edge to the segment in your design.

Place your line segment parallel to the horizontal lines of the Line-Divider™. Slide it until the segment endpoints lie on two division lines which have the desired number of units between them (Figure 1 and 2).

If the required unit on the segment must be longer than the bottom unit on the Line-Divider™, place your segment where you can mark it with twice the required number of units. Then mark every other division line to divide the segment into the required number of units (Figure 3).

If your line segment is too long to fit the Line-Divider™, bisect the segment and lightly mark the required number of units on each half of the segment. Then mark every other division line to divide the segment into the required number of units.

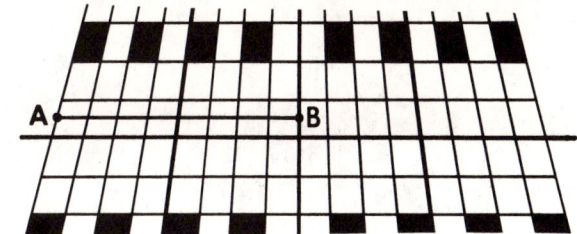

Example 1   8 division units

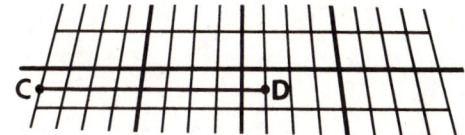

Example 2   9 division units

Example 3   3 division units

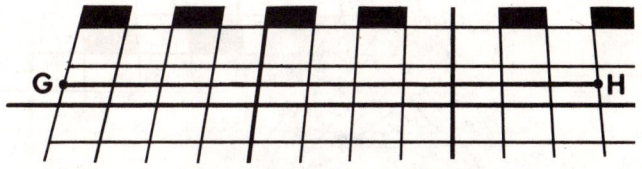

Example 4   11 division units

Line Designs

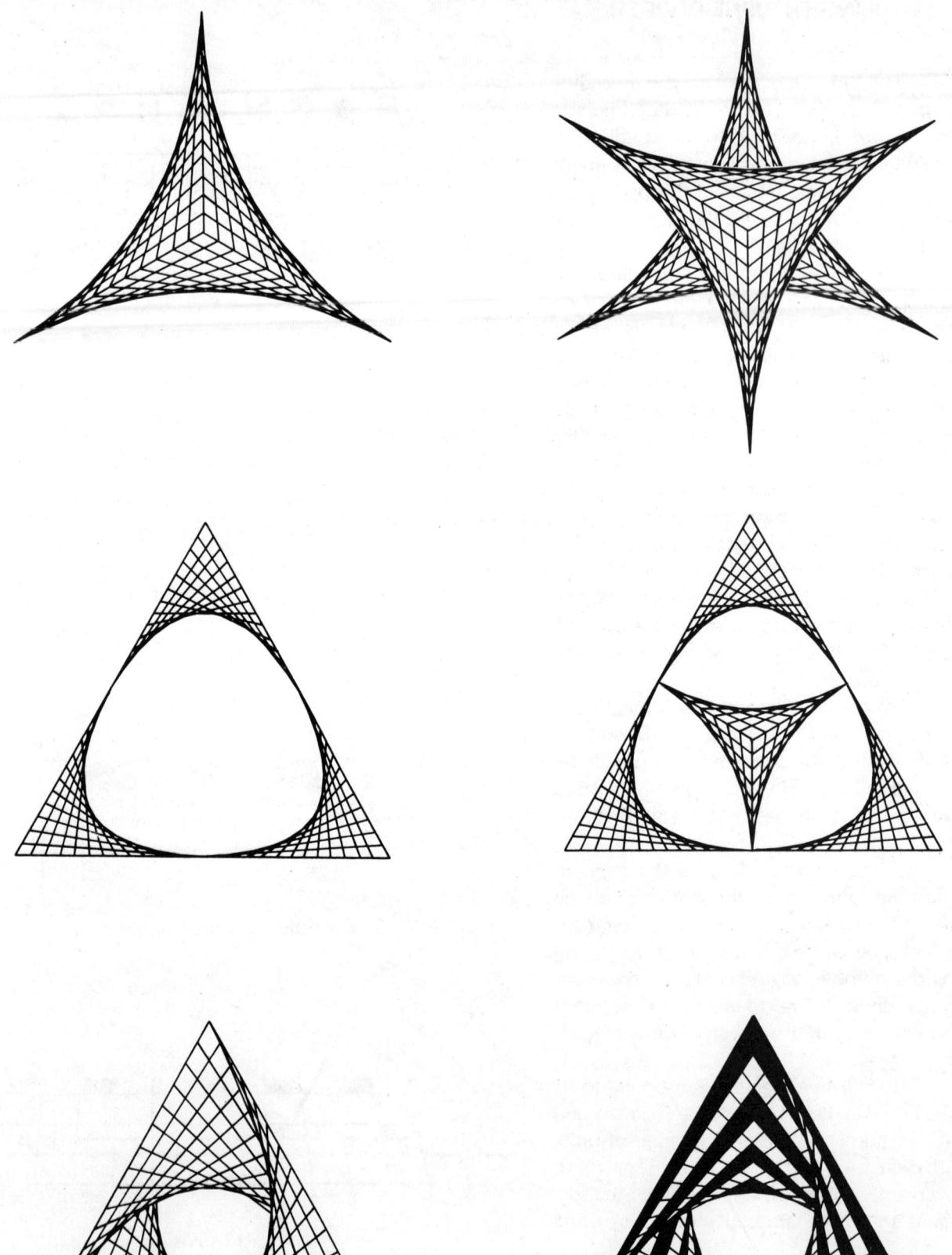

Line Designs 22 ©Ideal School Supply Company

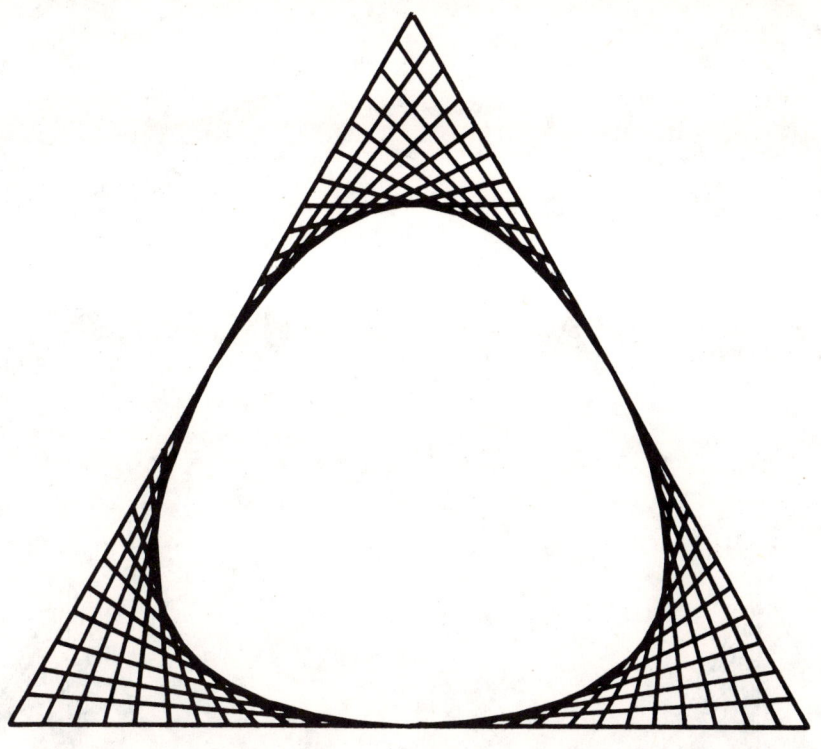

CONSTRUCT THIS DESIGN IN THE TRIANGLE BELOW

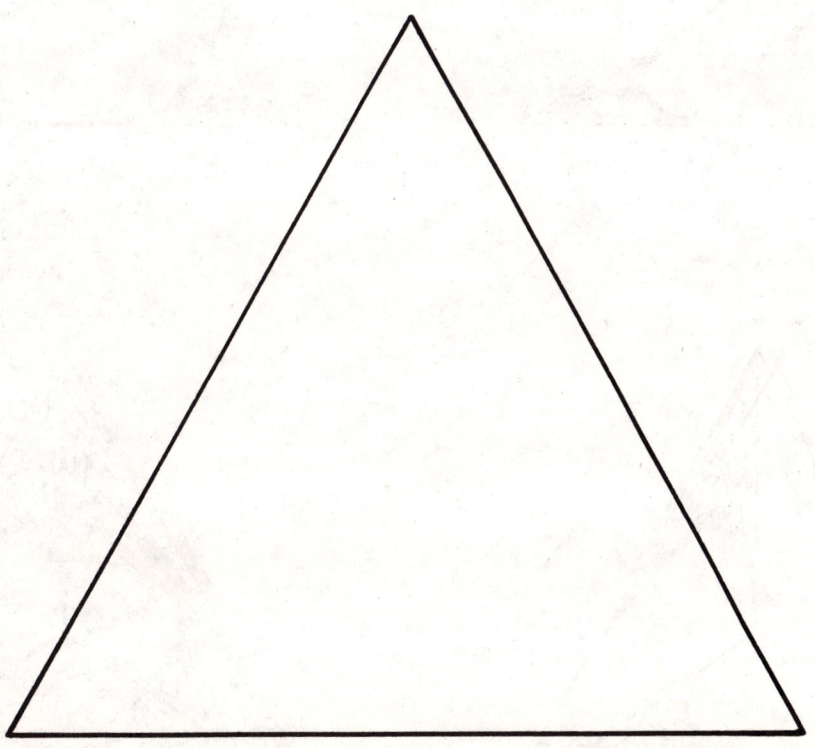

Line Designs

Line Designs

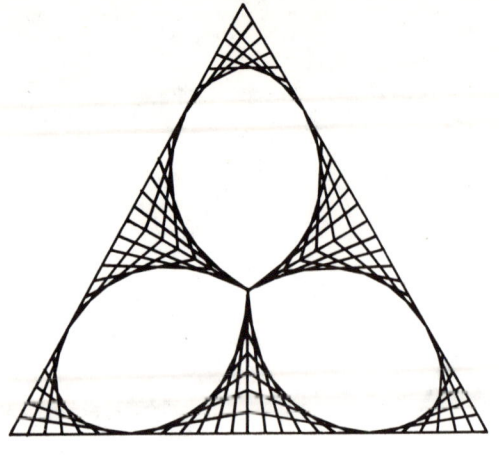

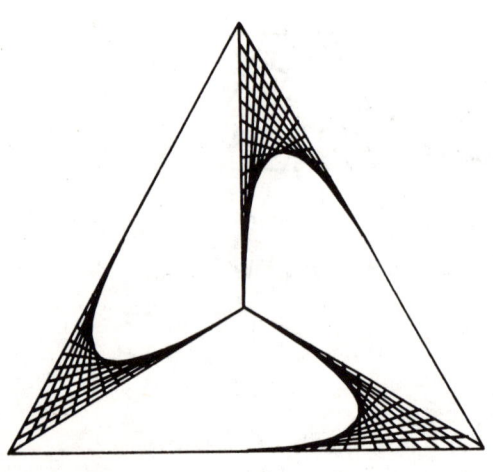
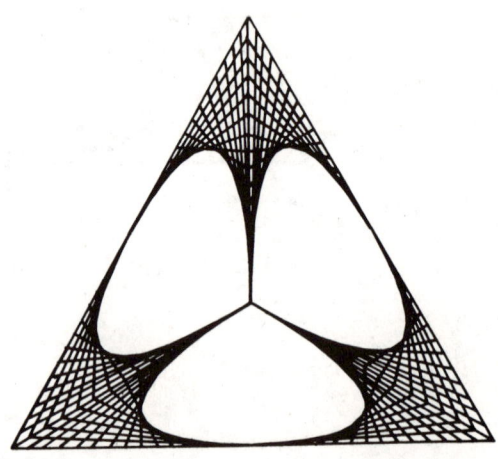
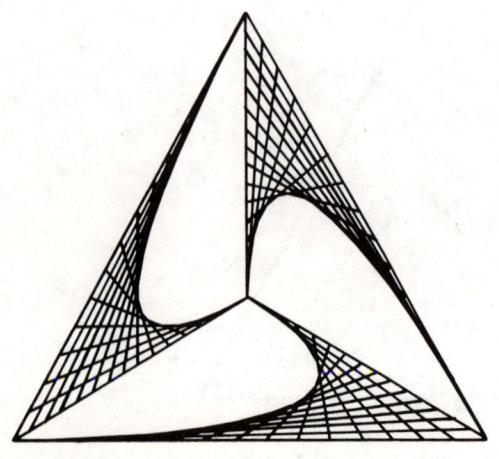
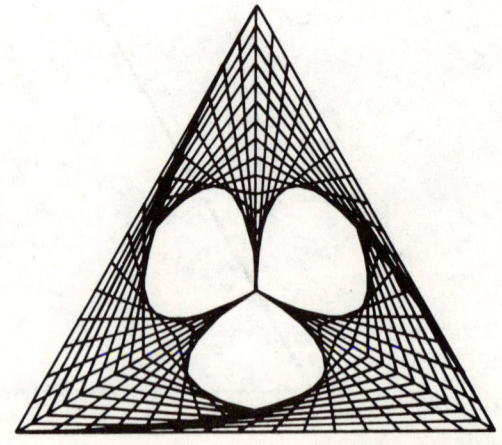

©Ideal School Supply Company

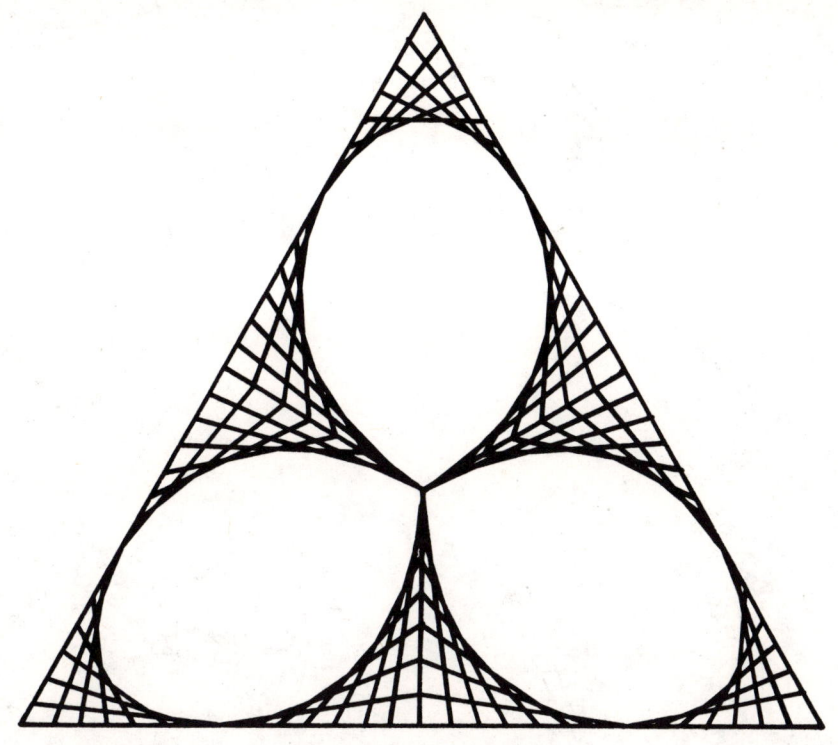

CONSTRUCT THIS DESIGN IN THE TRIANGLE BELOW

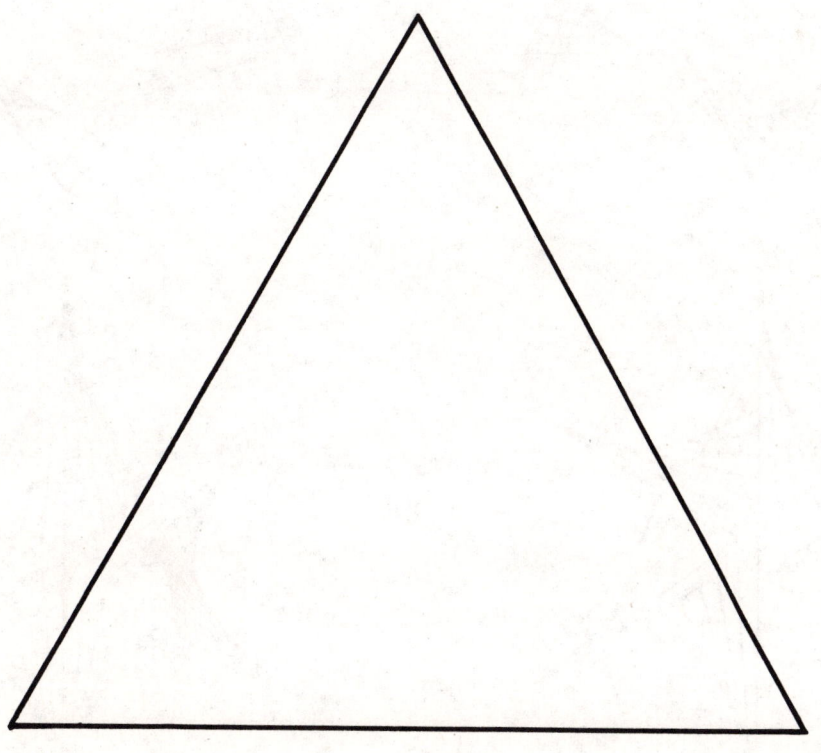

Line Designs

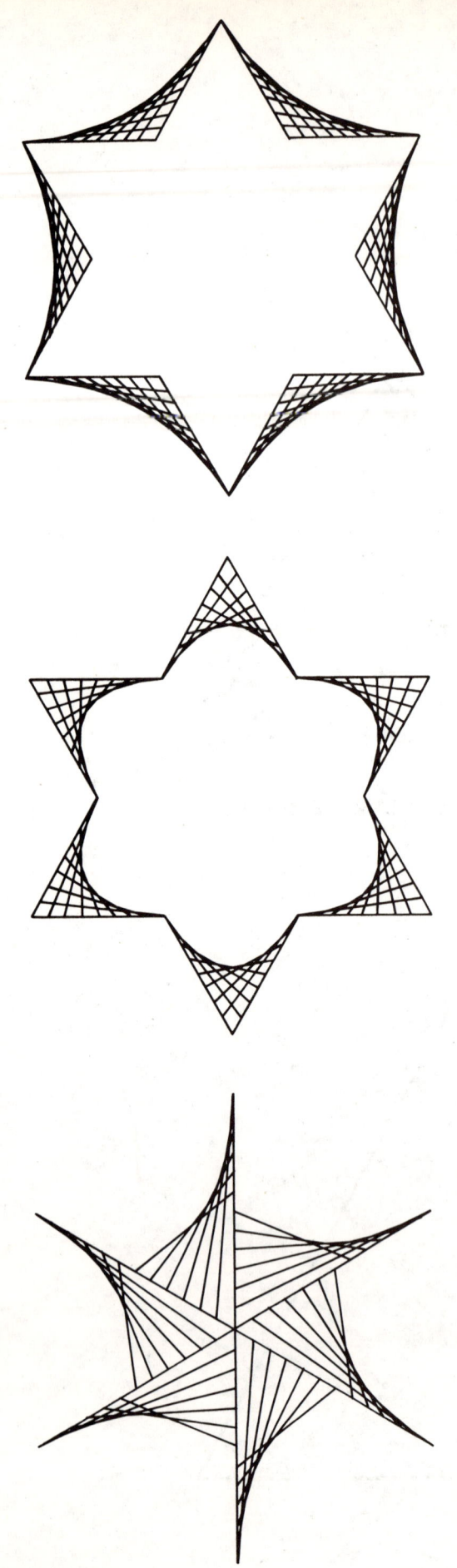
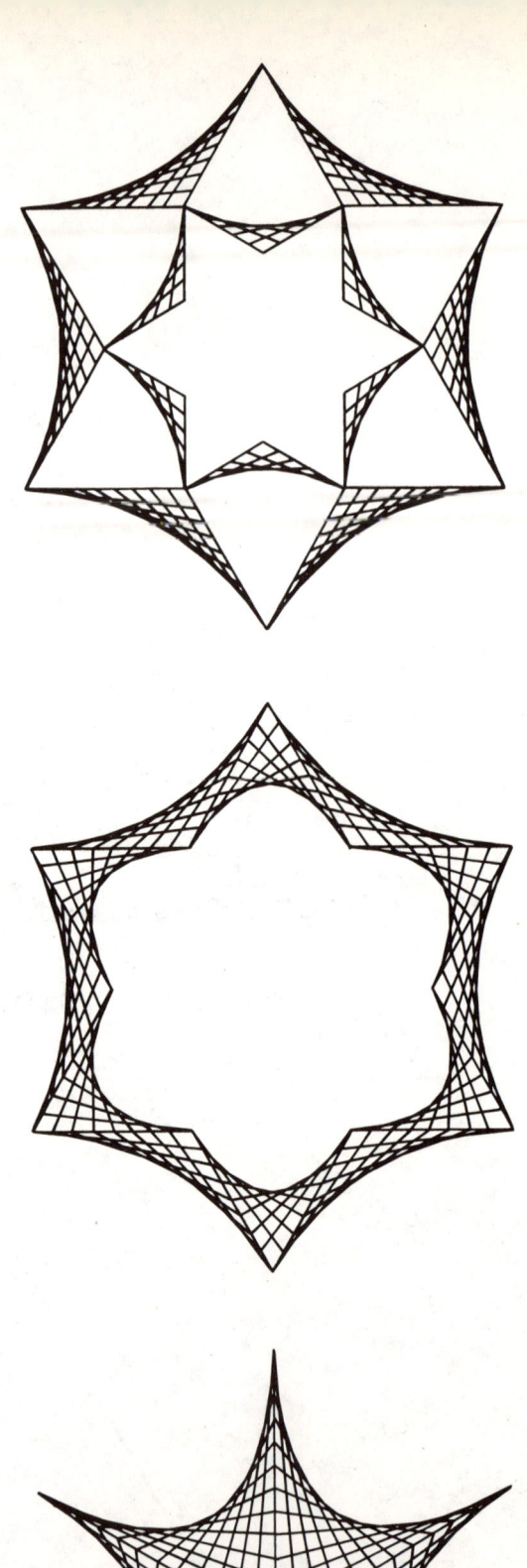
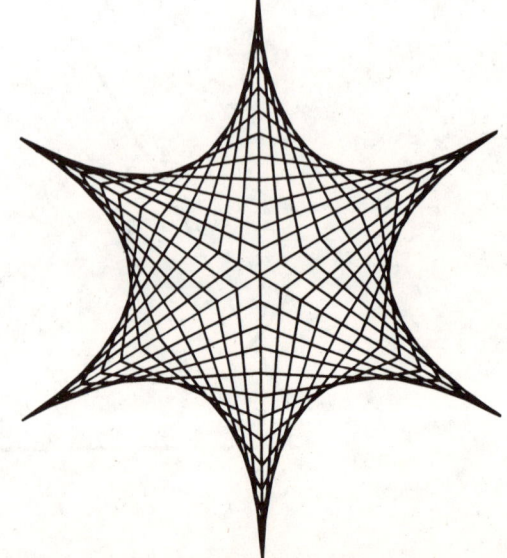

Line Designs
26
©Ideal School Supply Company

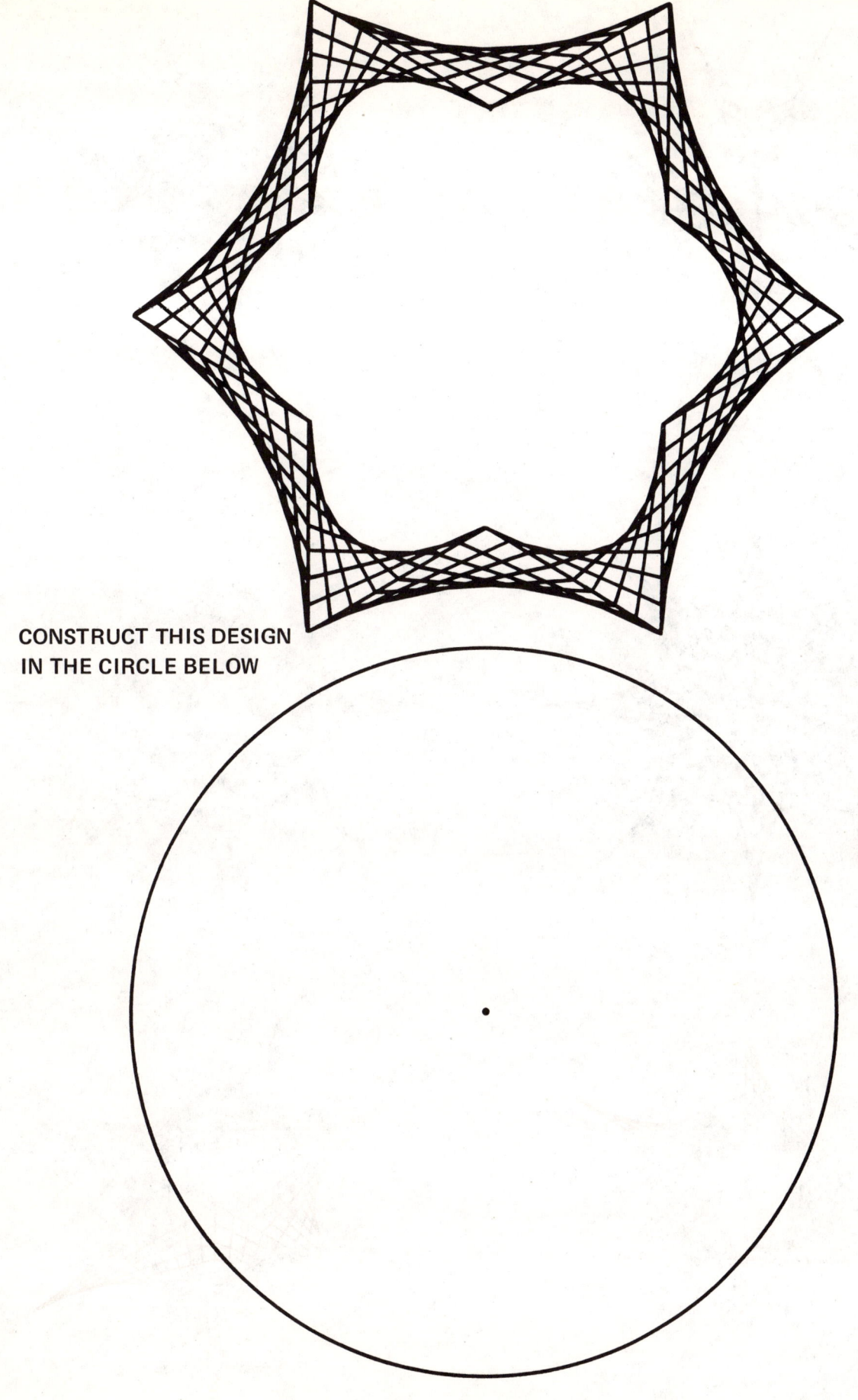

CONSTRUCT THIS DESIGN IN THE CIRCLE BELOW

Line Designs 27 ©Ideal School Supply Company

Line Designs

28

©Ideal School Supply Company

CONSTRUCT THIS DESIGN IN THE CIRCLE BELOW

Line Designs

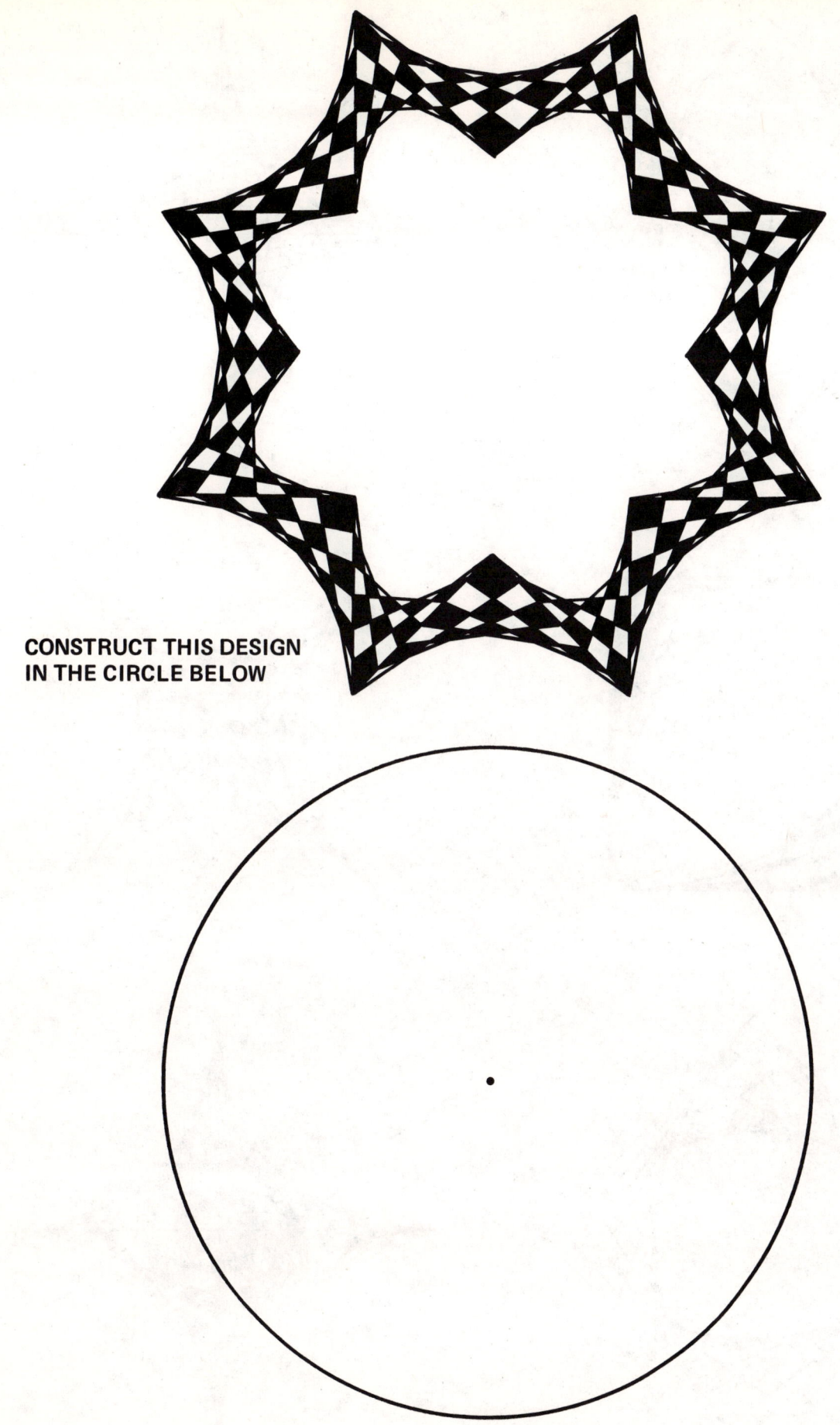

CONSTRUCT THIS DESIGN IN THE CIRCLE BELOW

Line Designs

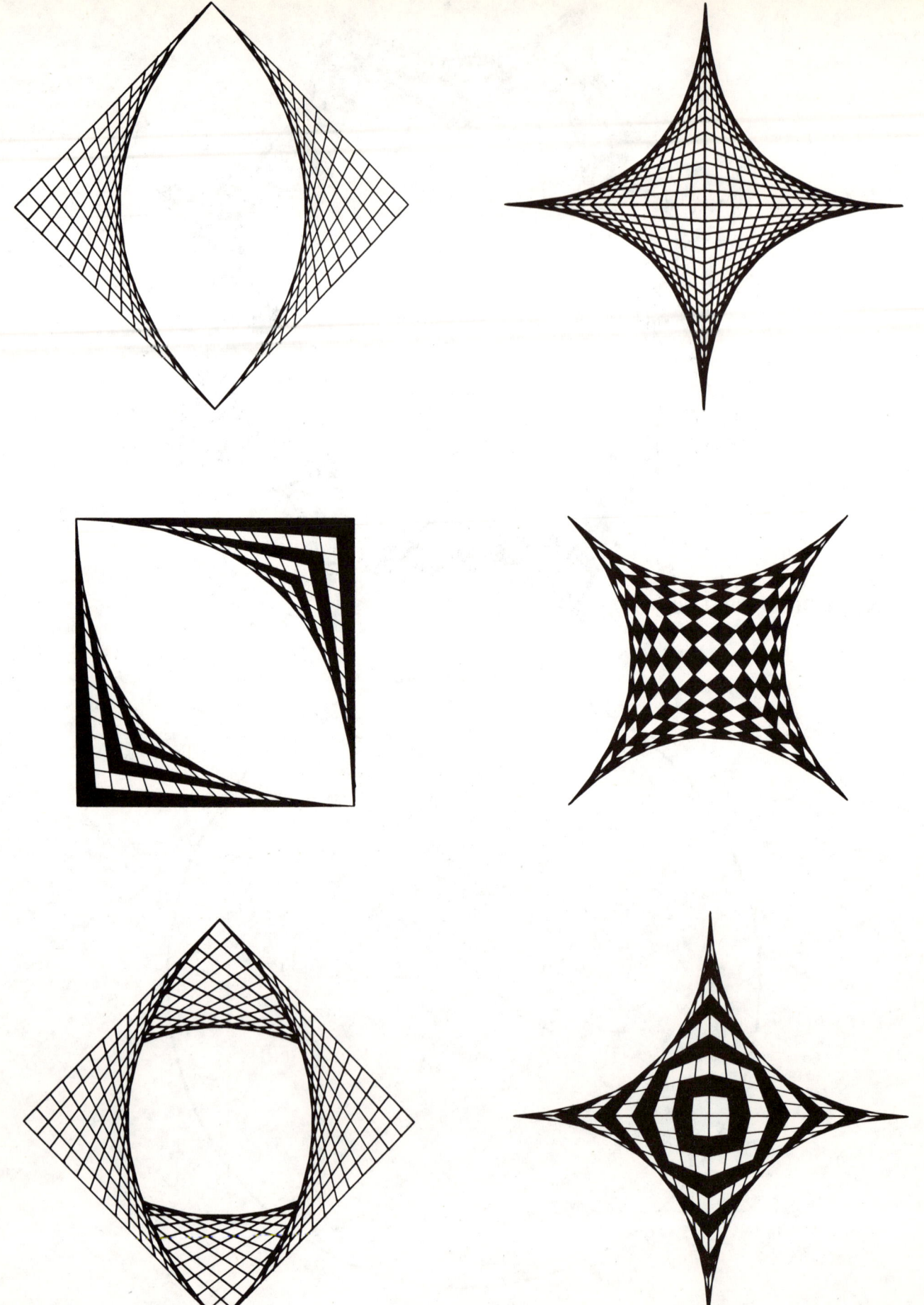

Line Designs   32   ©Ideal School Supply Company

CONSTRUCT THIS DESIGN IN THE SQUARE BELOW

Line Designs ©Ideal School Supply Company

Line Designs

34

©Ideal School Supply Company

CONSTRUCT THIS DESIGN IN THE SQUARE BELOW

Line Designs

Line Designs

36

©Ideal School Supply Company

CONSTRUCT THIS DESIGN IN THE SQUARE BELOW

Line Designs

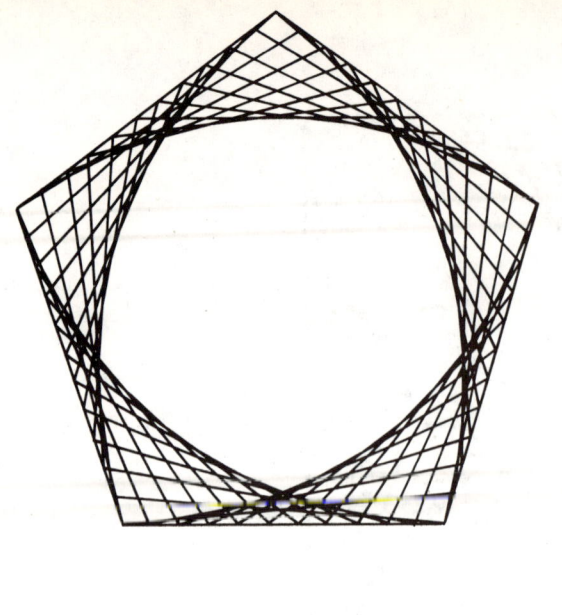 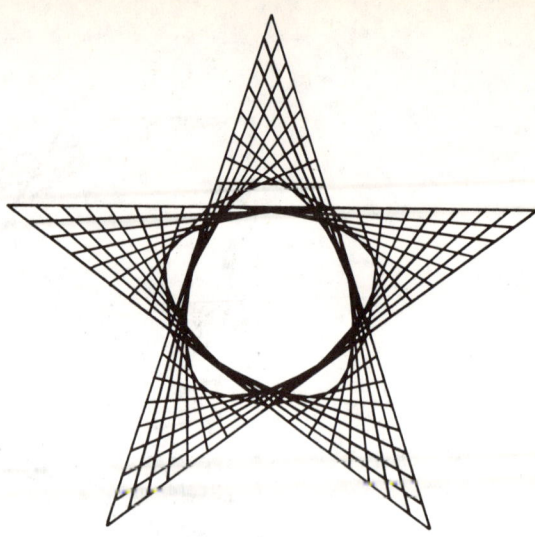
 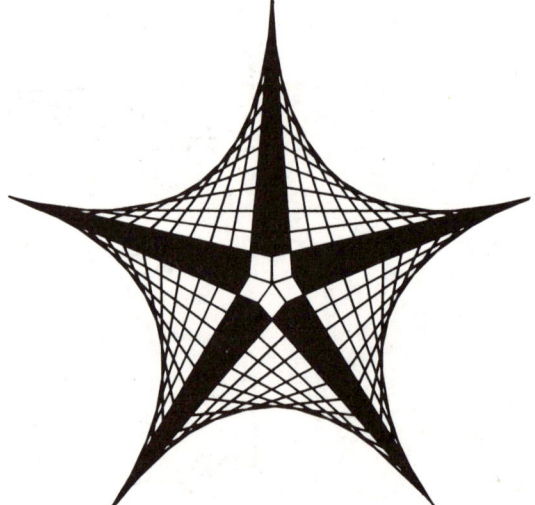
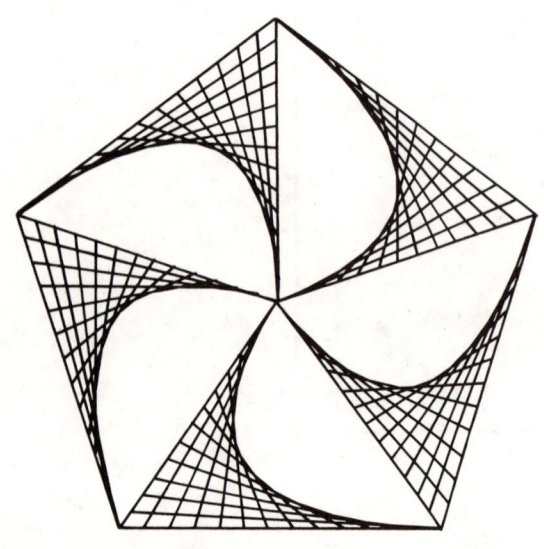 

Line Designs

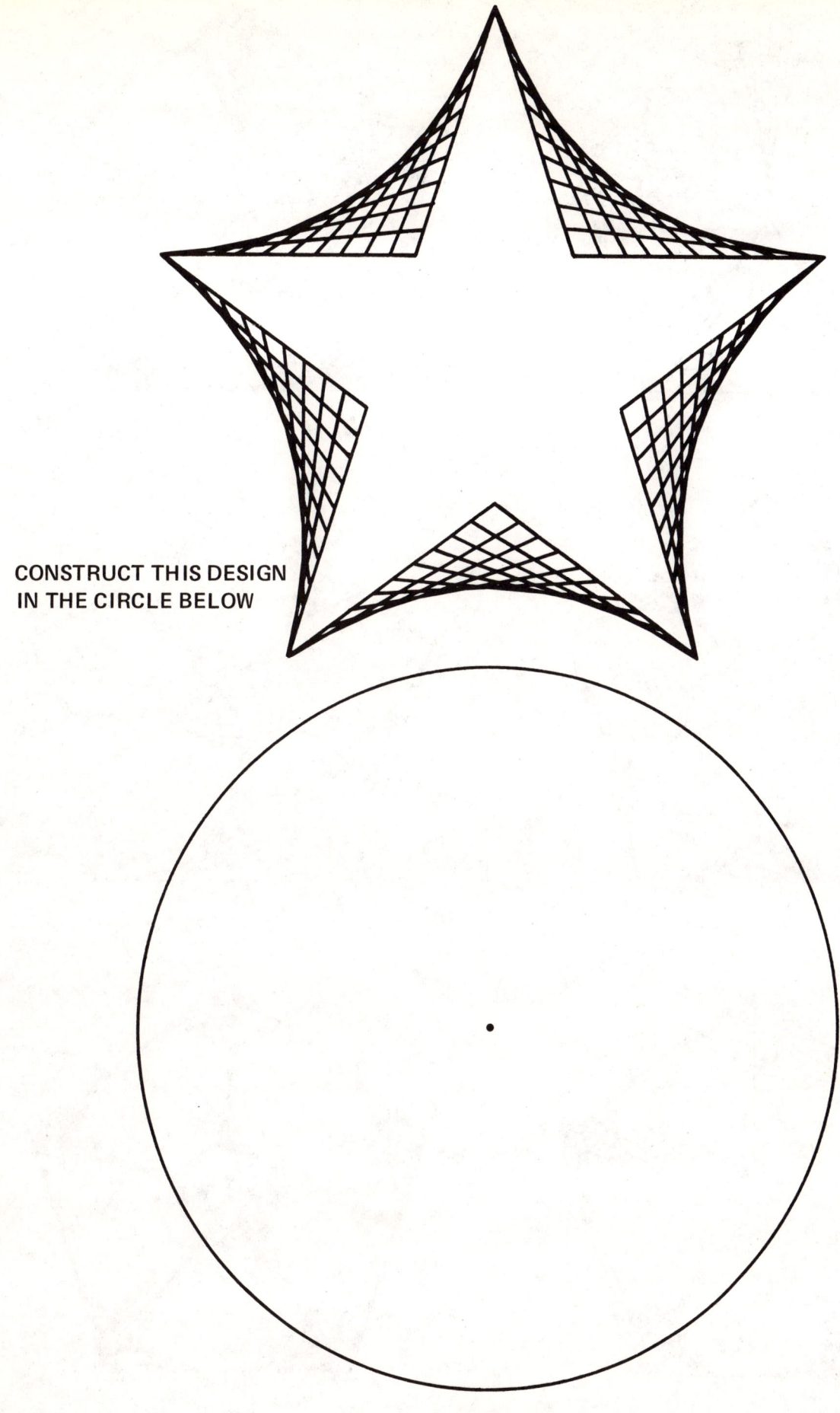

CONSTRUCT THIS DESIGN IN THE CIRCLE BELOW

Line Designs

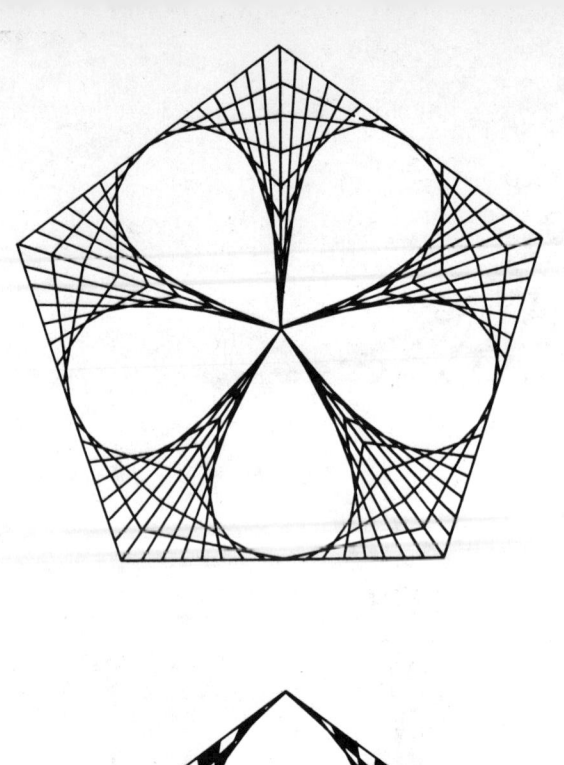
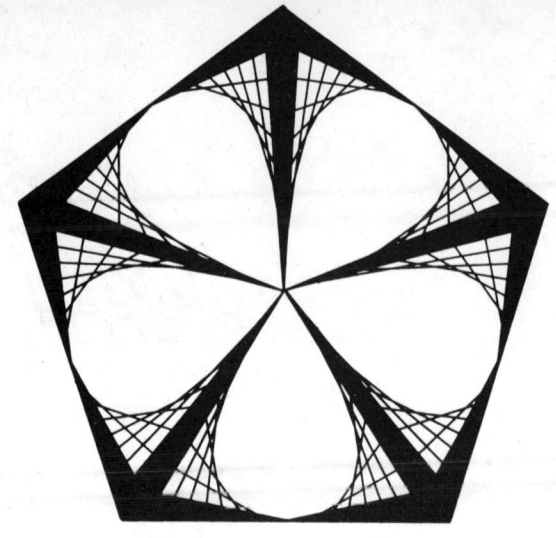

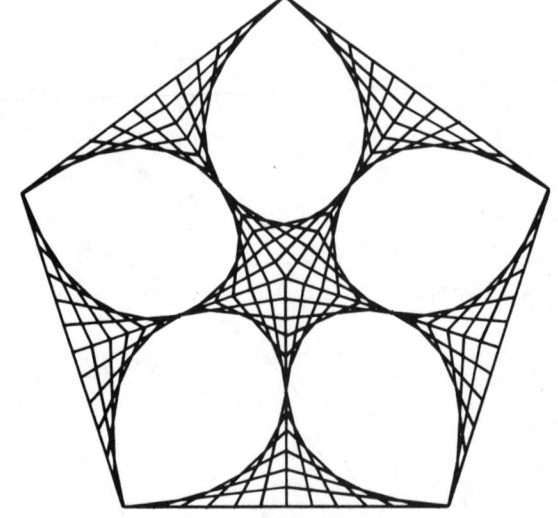

Line Designs

40

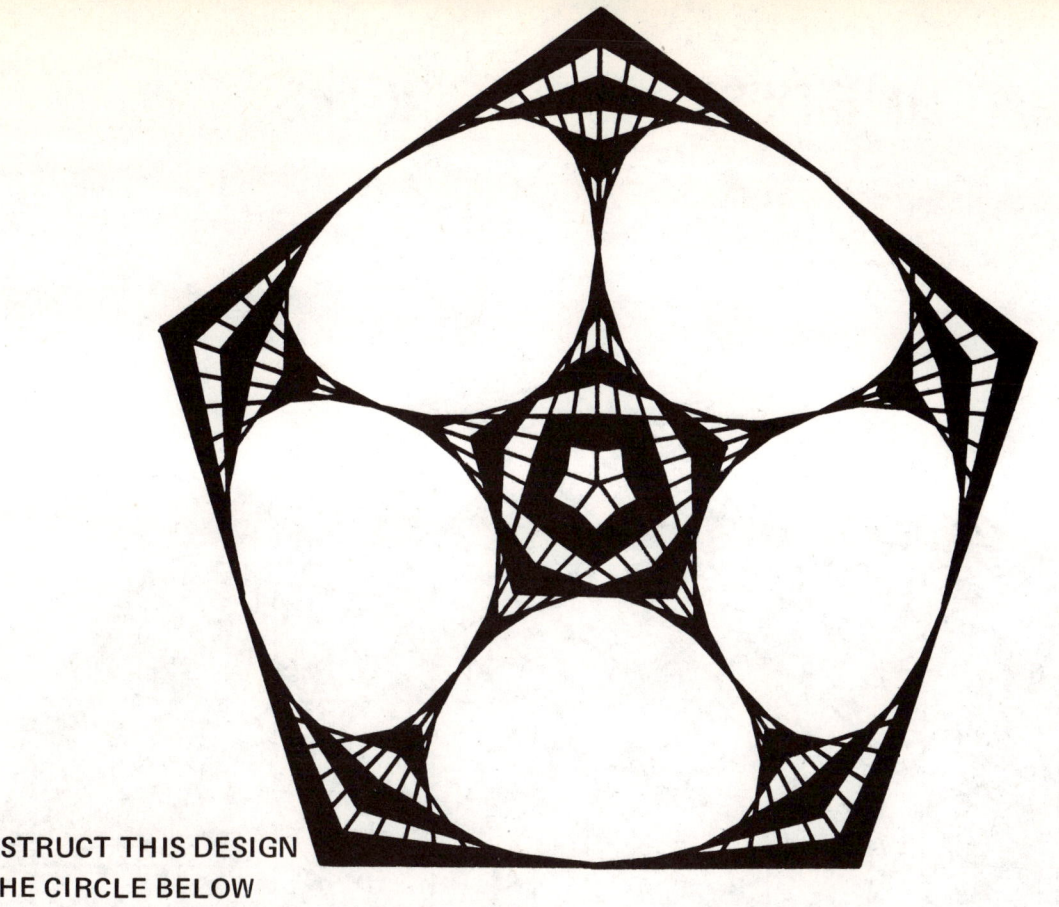

CONSTRUCT THIS DESIGN IN THE CIRCLE BELOW

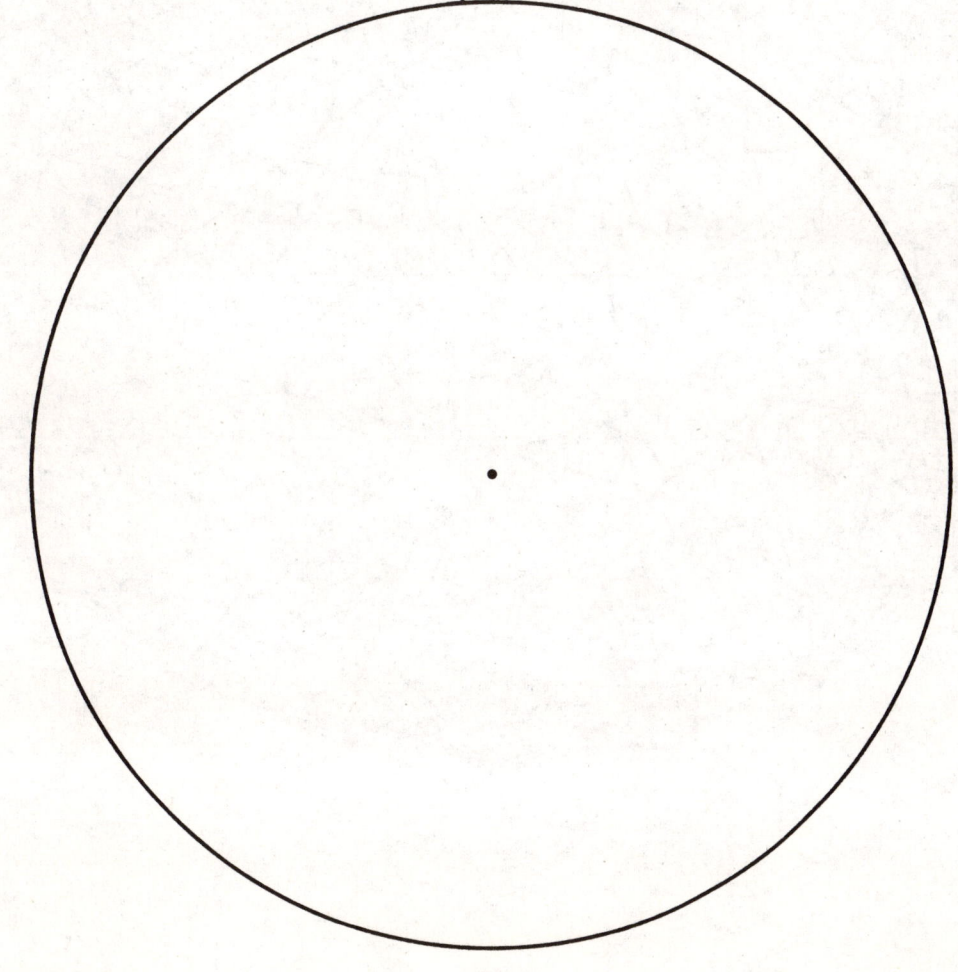

Line Designs

LINE DESIGNS IN CIRCLES

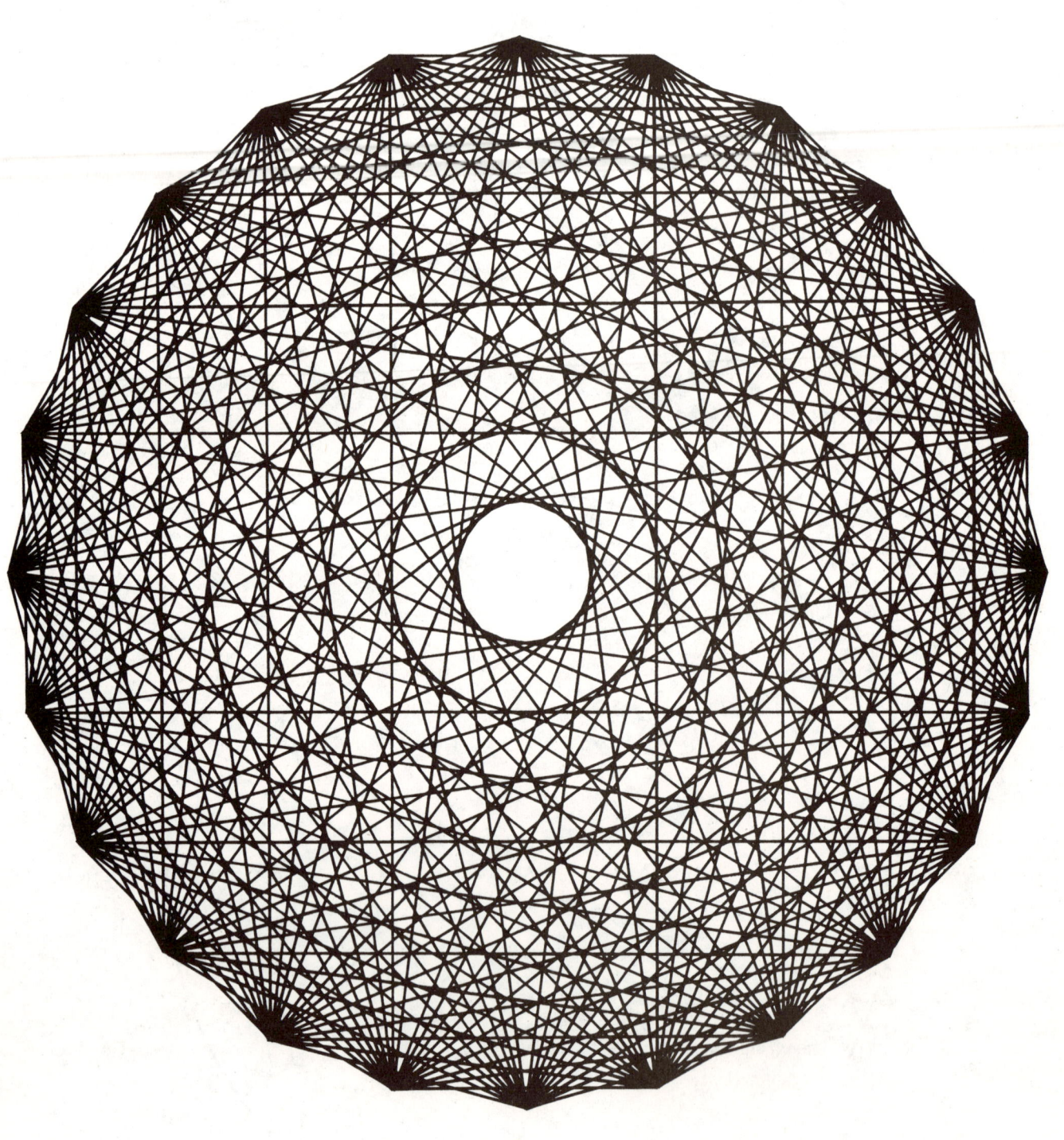

The line designs shown on this page were drawn by connecting equally-spaced points on circles with straight line segments. As is the case with designs having an angle as their base, an illusion of a curve is created by the straight lines. The three designs shown here are particularly effective in colored thread on a felt-covered board. Similar line designs can be made by connecting equally-spaced points on arcs or conics.

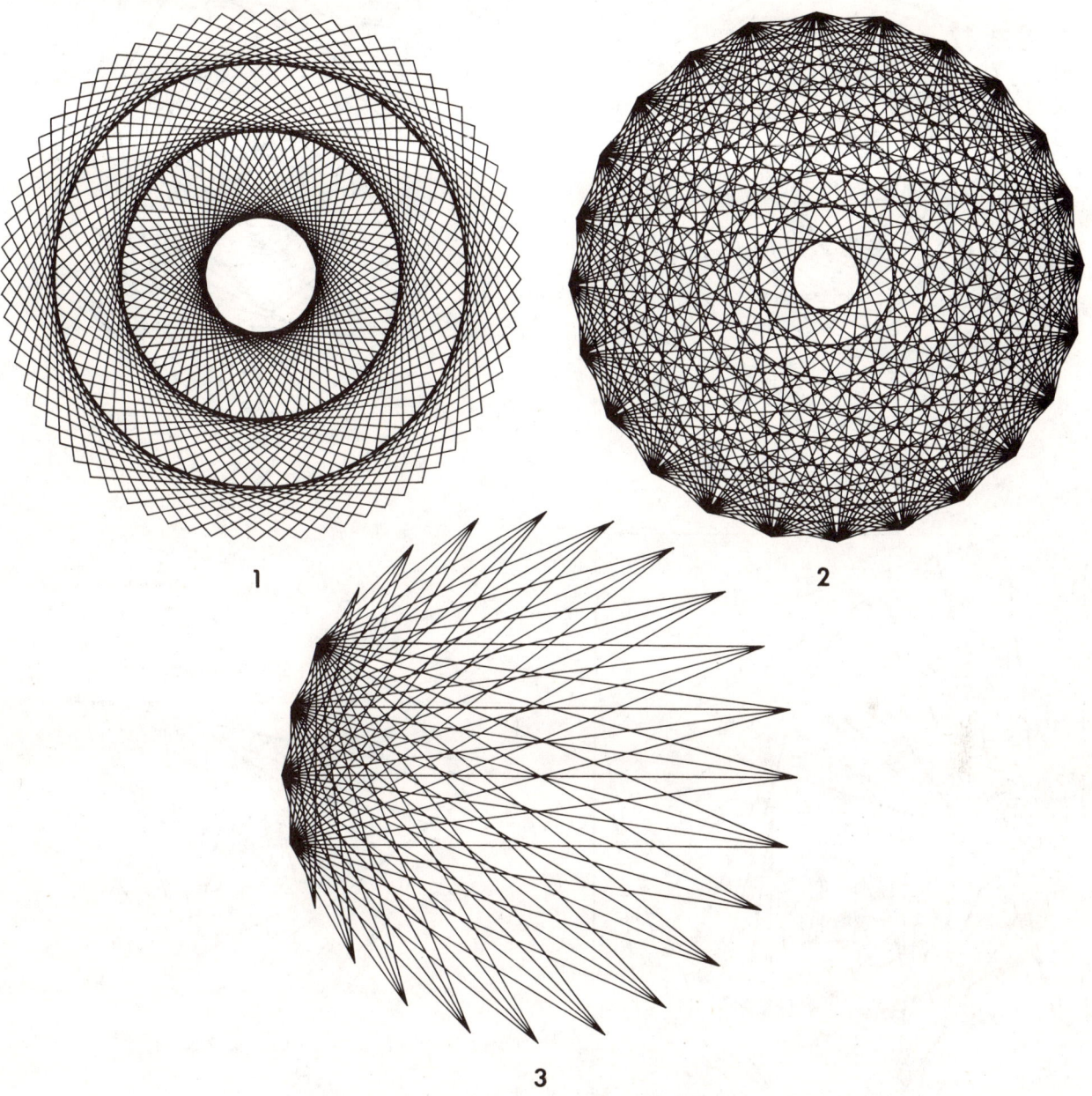

1

2

3

Figure 1   Twenty-four equally spaced points on a circle. Connect each point to every other point on the circle except the two adjacent to it and the one directly across the circle.

Figure 2   Seventy-two points on a circle (use polar grid paper). Outer ring connects points 15 spaces apart. Second ring connects points twenty-three spaces apart. Inner ring connects points 31 spaces apart.

Figure 3   Twenty-four points on a circle. Four of them are connected to all points except the two on either side of them.

Line Designs   ©Ideal School Supply Company

LINE DESIGN SPIRALS

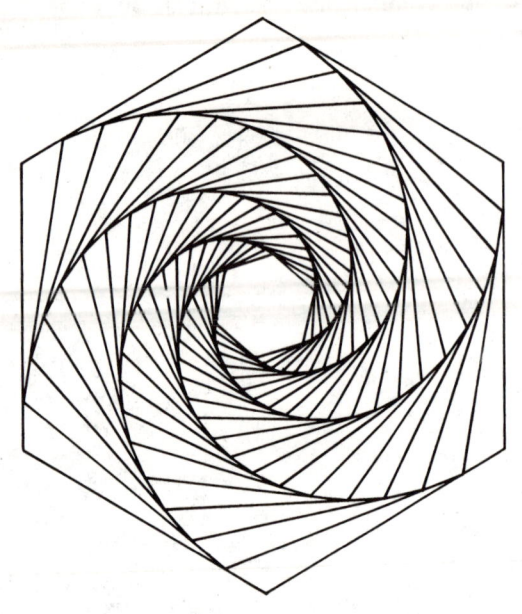
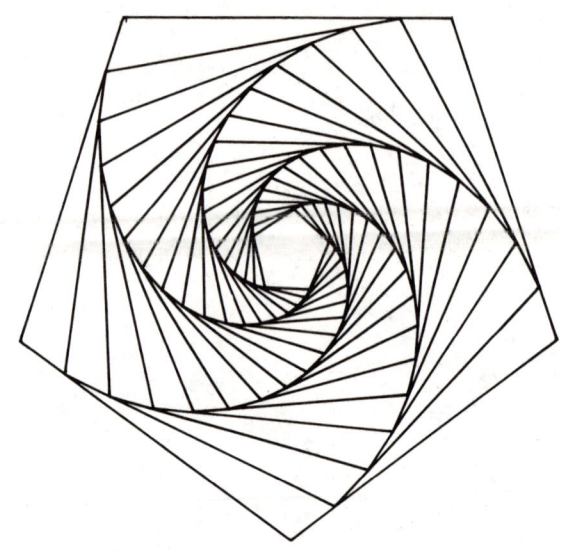
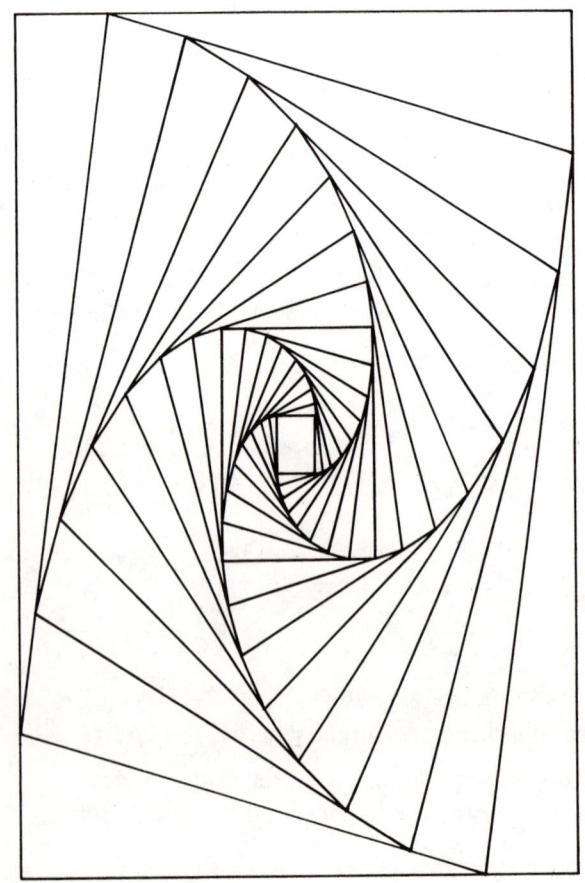
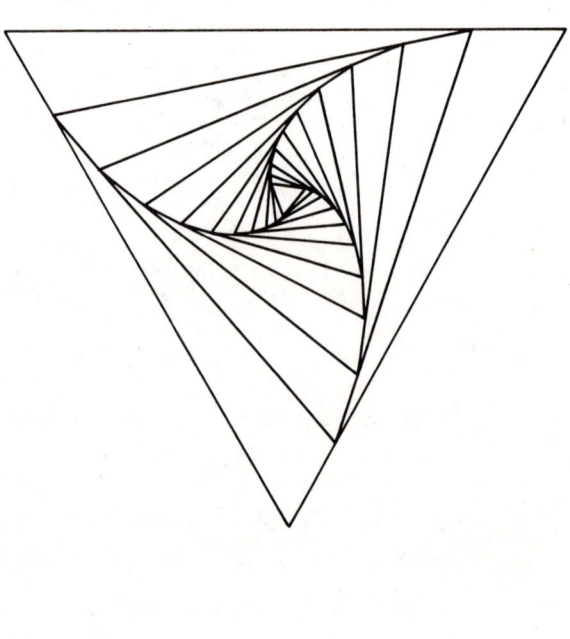

LINE DESIGN SPIRALS

The drawings on the previous page appear to contain spiral curves. These curves are an illusion since all lines in the figures are line segments. The general technique for creating these designs is described below and illustrated at the right.

STEP 1. Mark a point on each side of the square one sixth of the length of the side (Figure 1).

STEP 2. Connect points on adjacent sides of the square. The result is a smaller square (Figure 2).

STEP 3. Repeat step 1 above on square ABCD (Figure 3).

STEP 4. Repeat step 2 above (Figure 4).

STEP 5. Continue the procedure until you achieve the desired result (Figure 5).

The closer together the points on the side of the square the more evident the spiral. You may wish to divide the side of the square into units other than one sixth. The Line-Divider™ (page 20) will prove very helpful in making spiral line designs. Spirals in other polygons are achieved in the same manner as the spiral in the square.

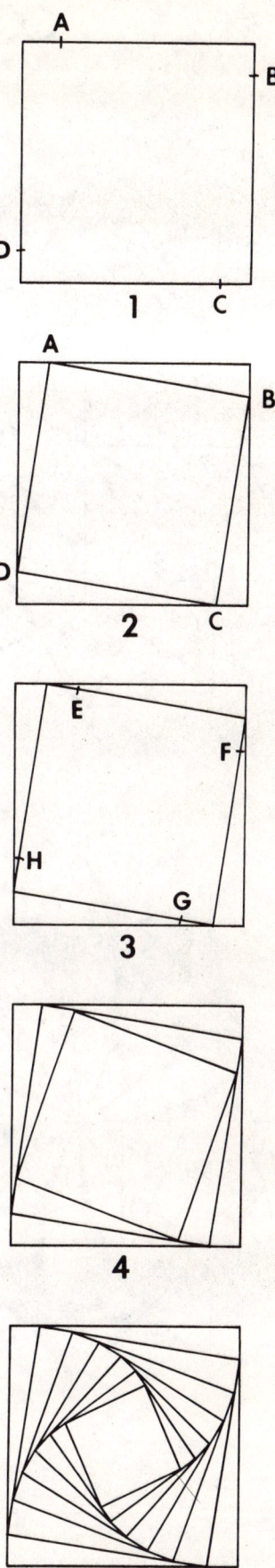

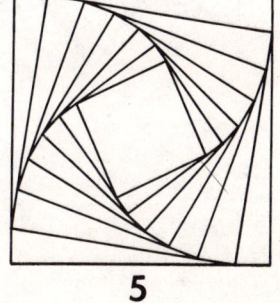

Line Designs

COMPLEX LINE DESIGNS

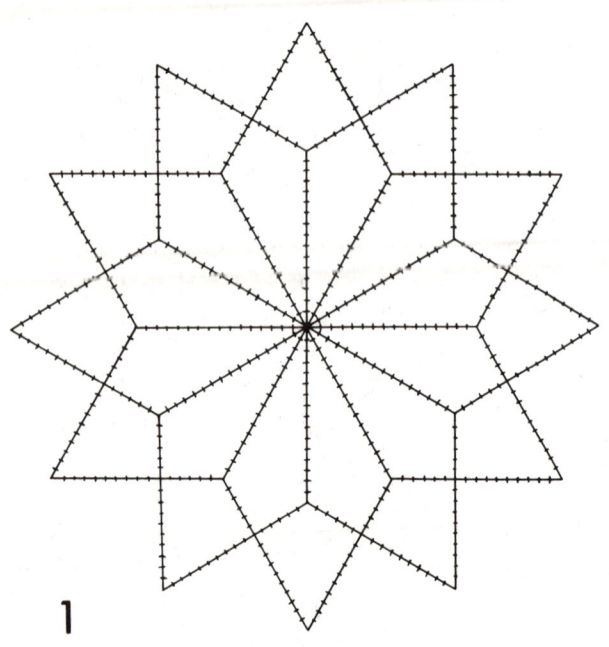

1

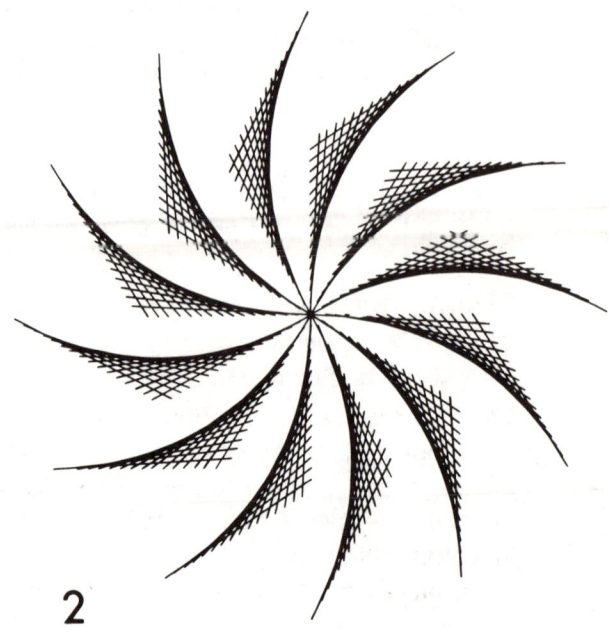

2

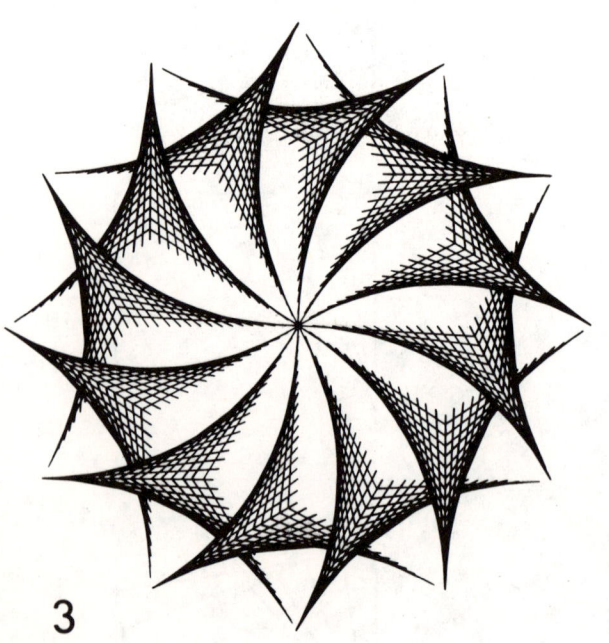

3

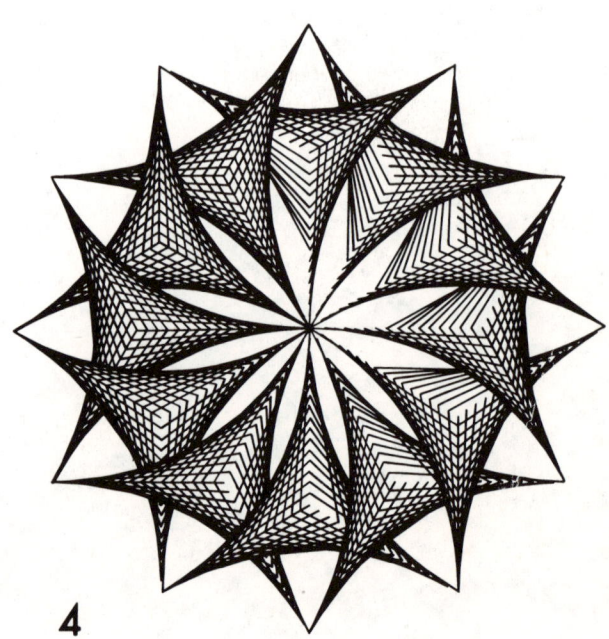

4

Line Designs ©Ideal School Supply Company

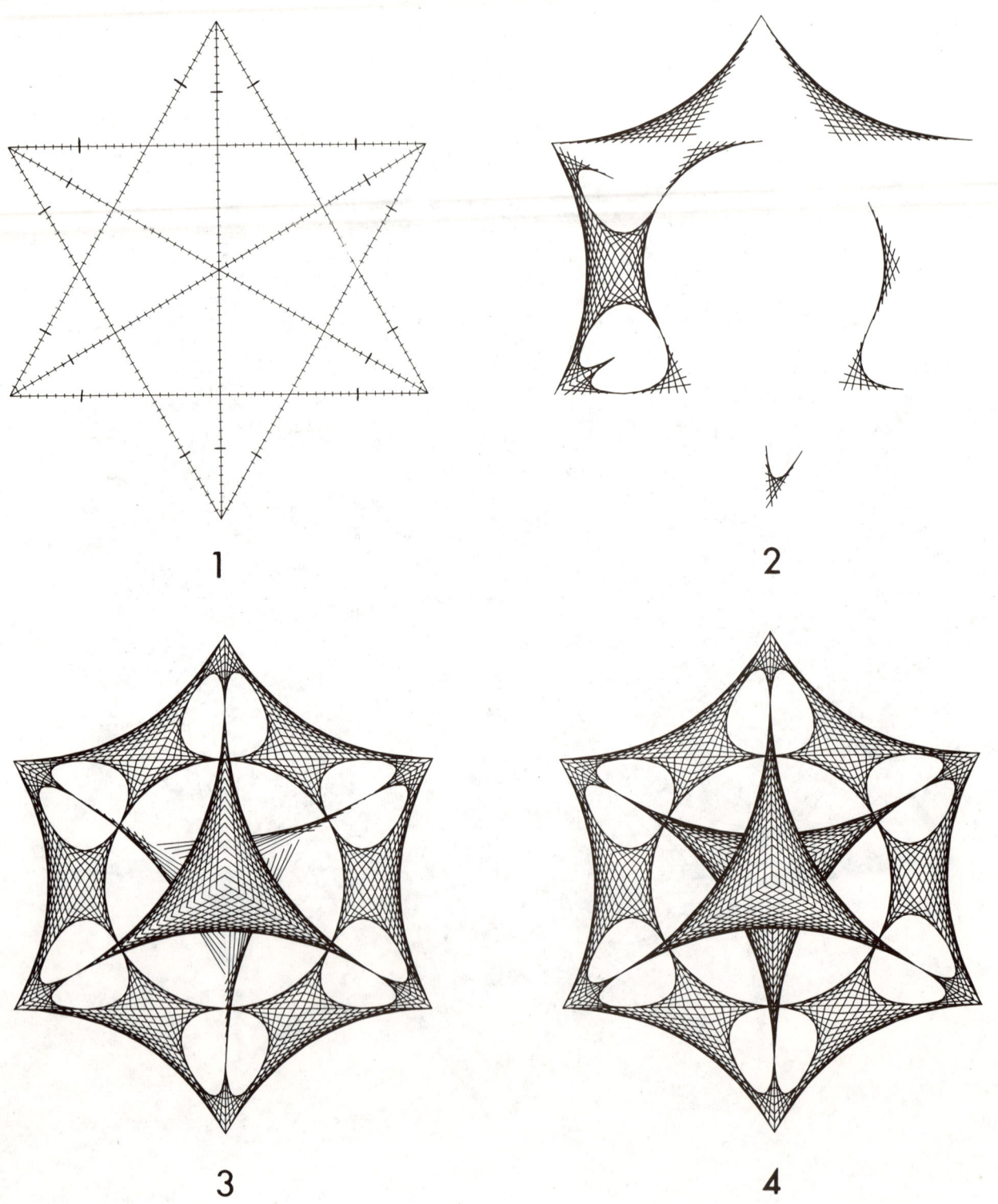

Line Designs

48

©Ideal School Supply Company

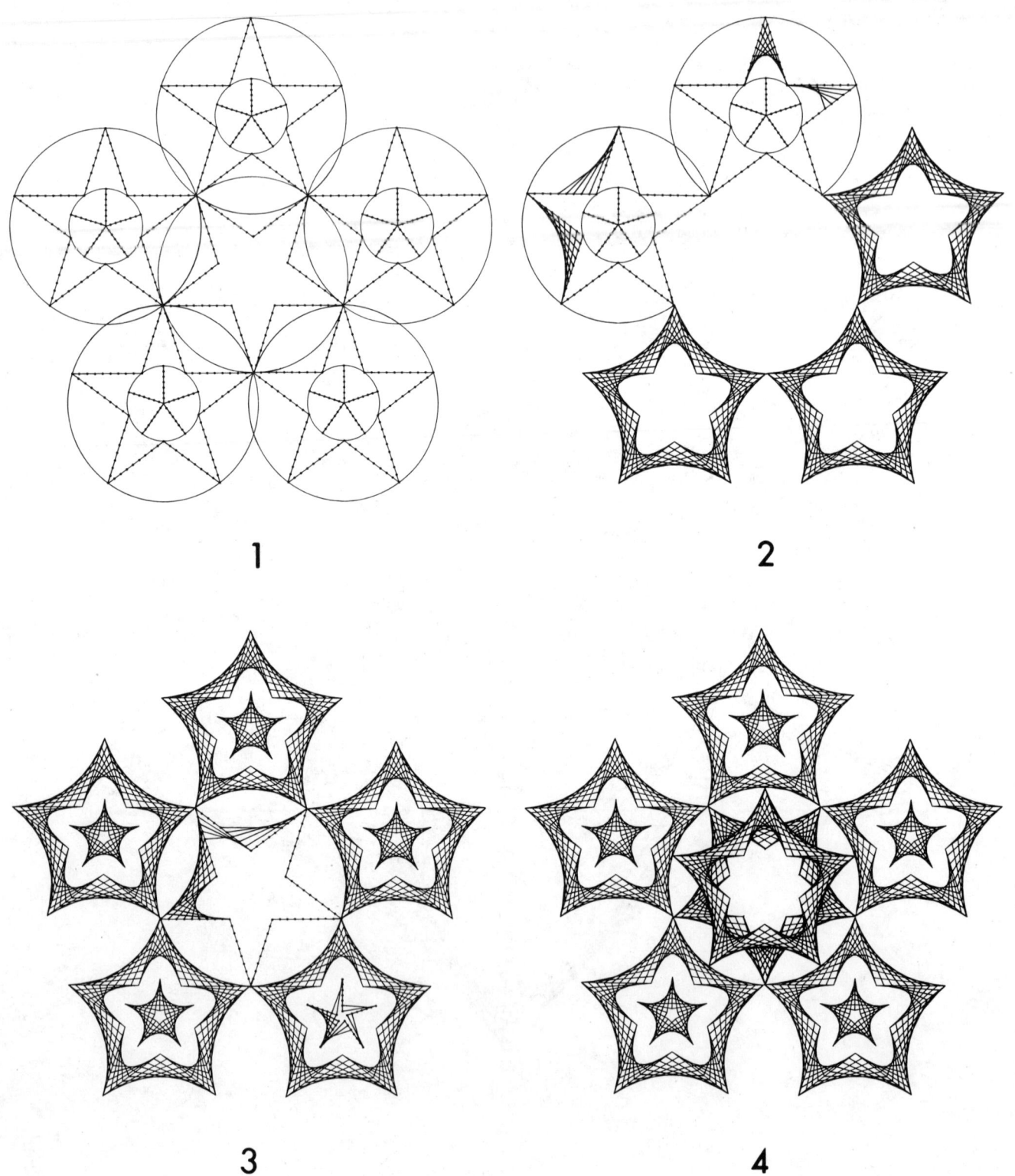

Line Designs

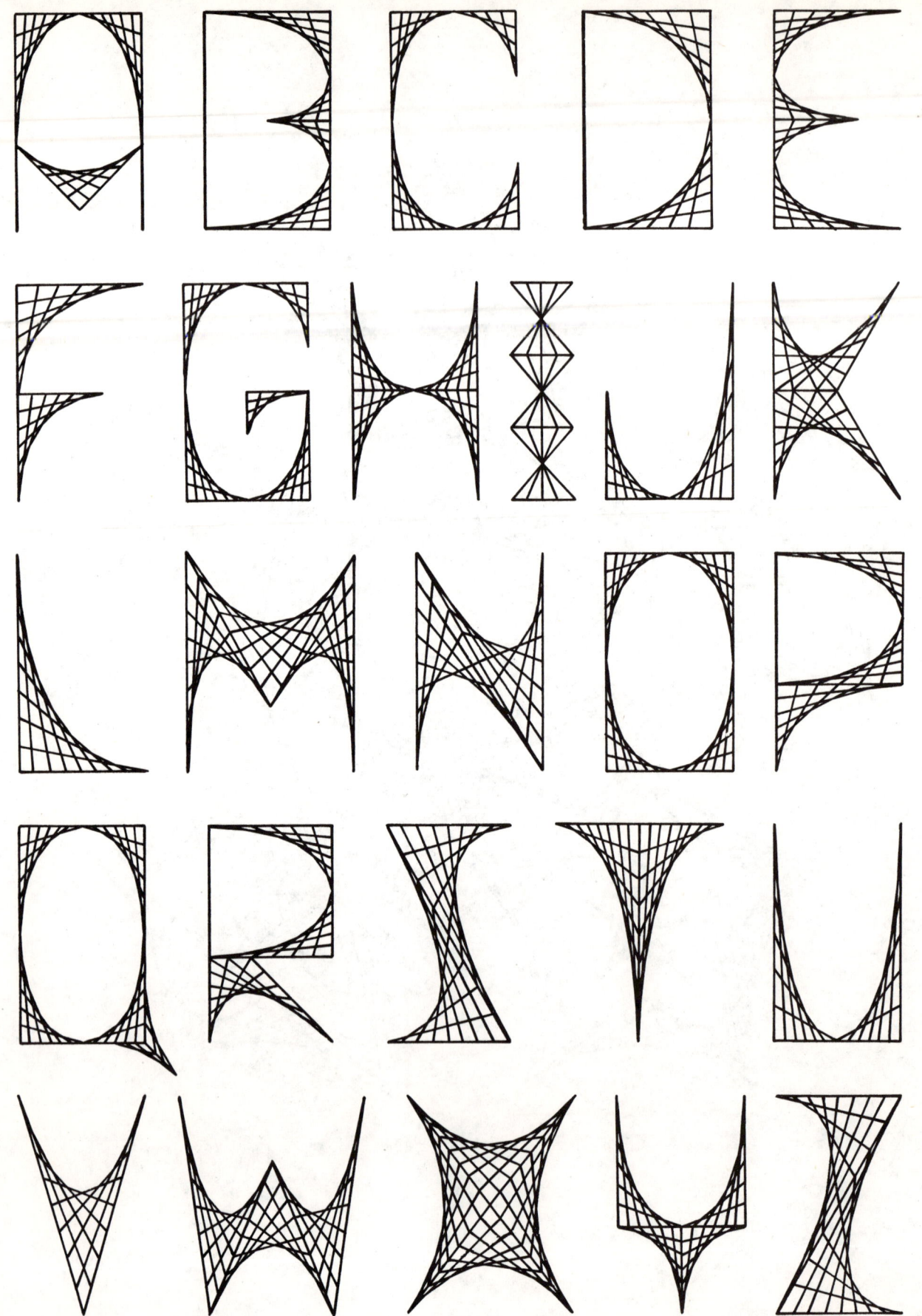

Line Designs ©Ideal School Supply Company

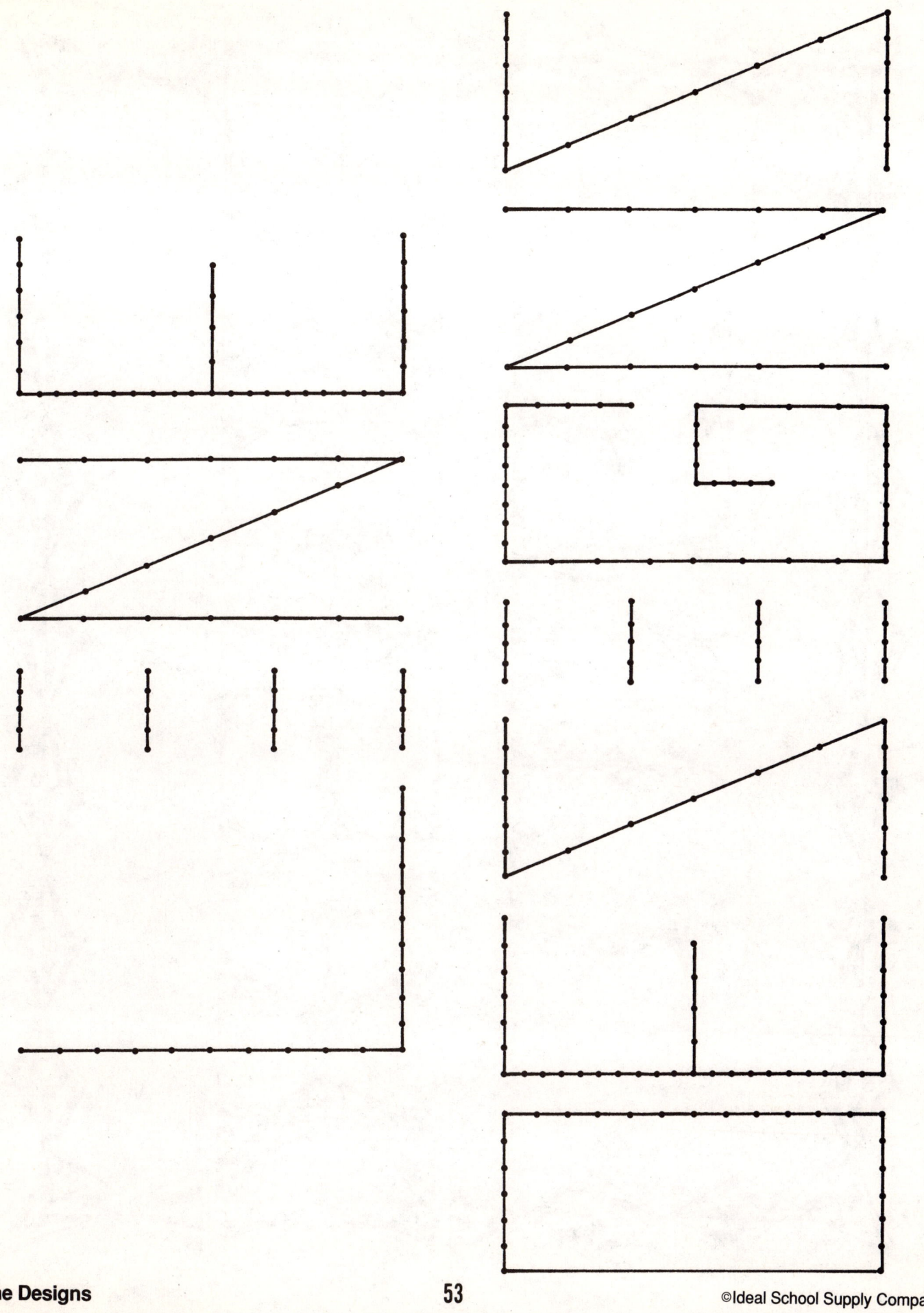

Line Designs

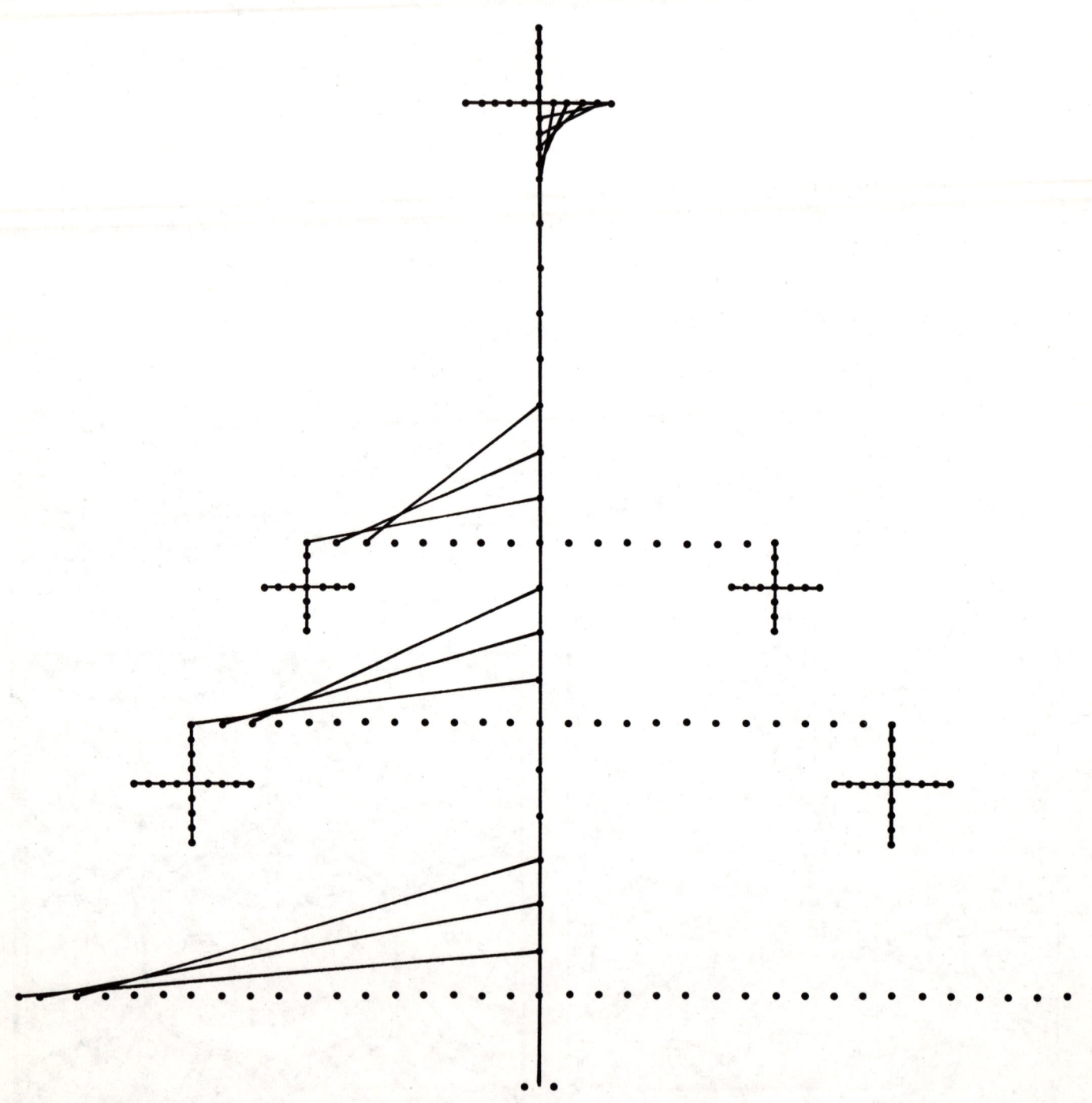

Line Designs

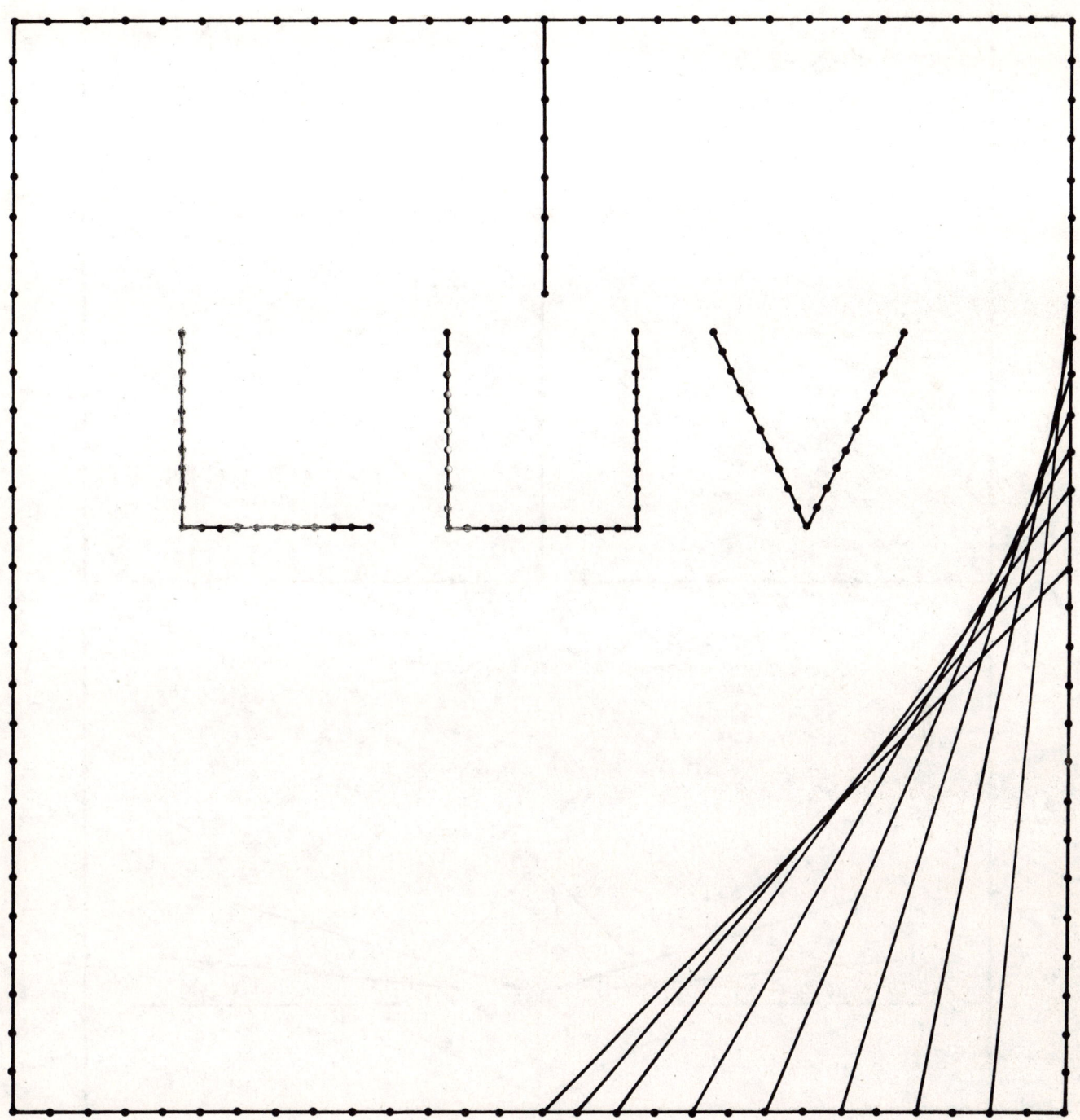

Line Designs

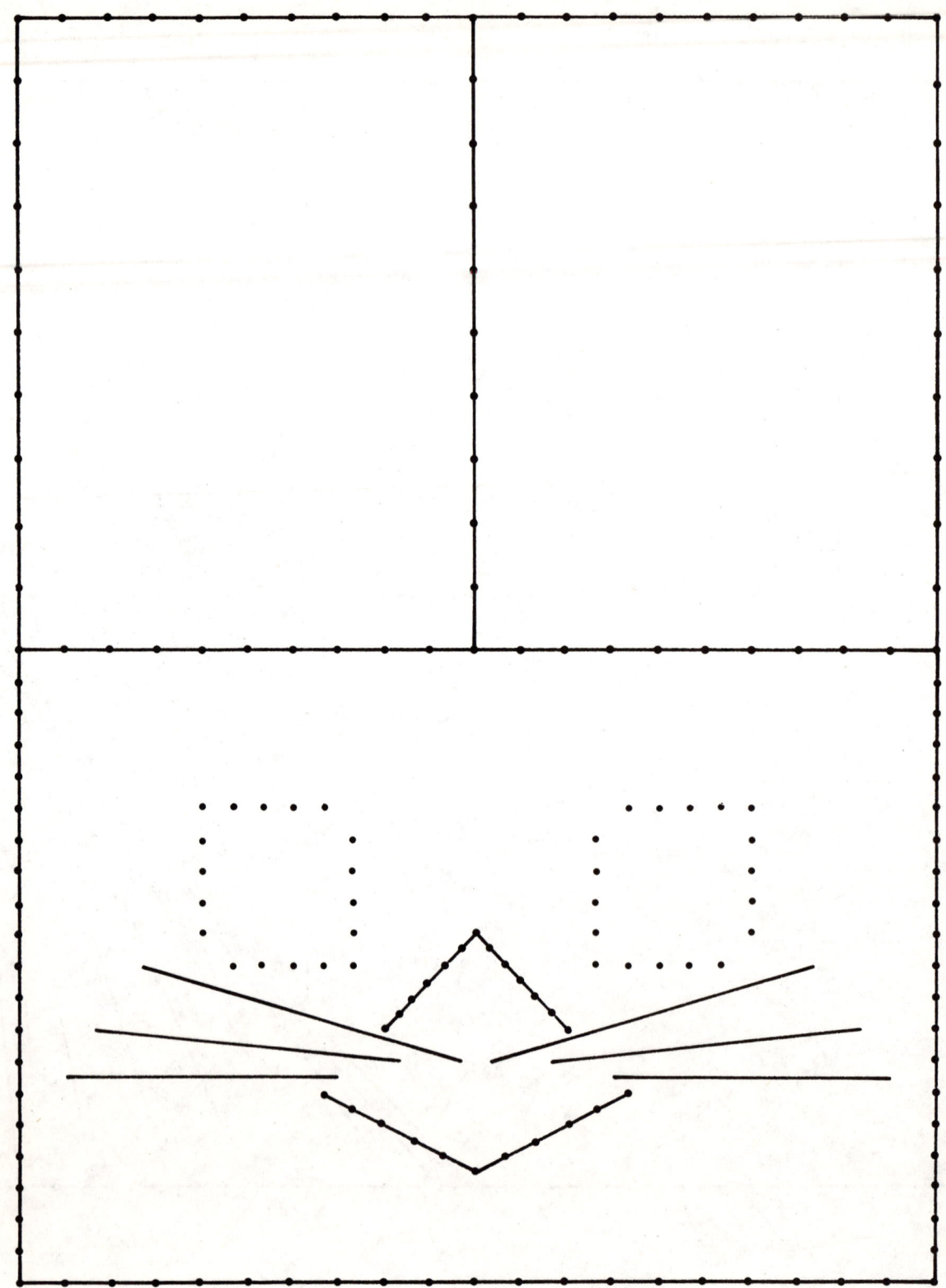

Line Designs

58

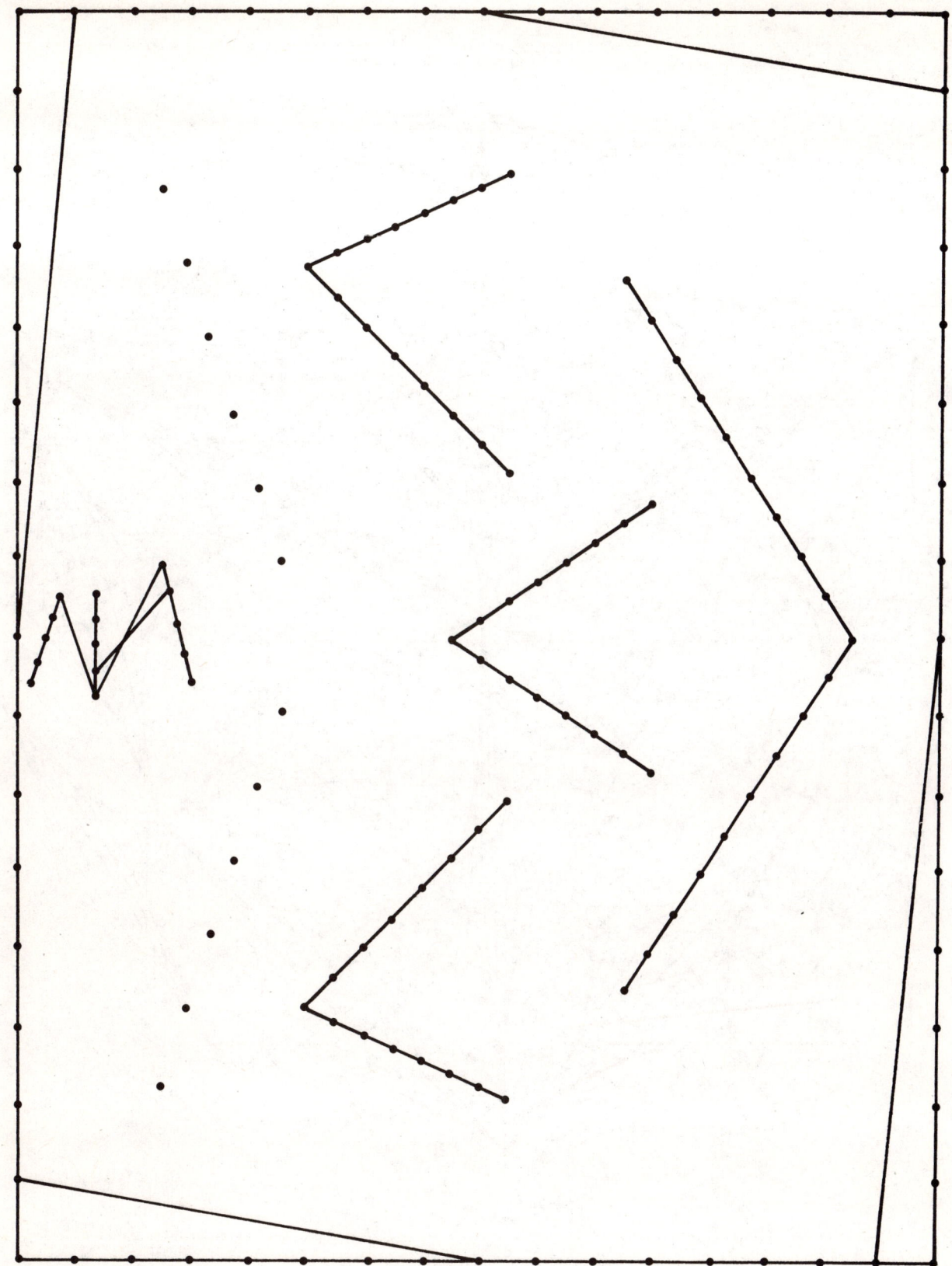

Line Designs

LINE DESIGN MOSAICS

You can make beautiful geometric patterns by combining several simple line designs. This page is an example of a partial tessellation (plane filling) of line designs based on a square. This design could repeat infinitely in a plane. One effective way to create line design mosaics is with combinations of polygons which have congruent sides. Line designs created from six such shapes are shown on the next page. These designs were formed from the Pattern Block shapes which can be combined to make unlimited numbers of designs. You will be able to design complex and beautiful mosaics if you reproduce several copies of the Lined Link-Ups on page 62, cut out the designs, and then experiment with combinations of the Link-Ups.

Line Designs

LINED LINK-UPS

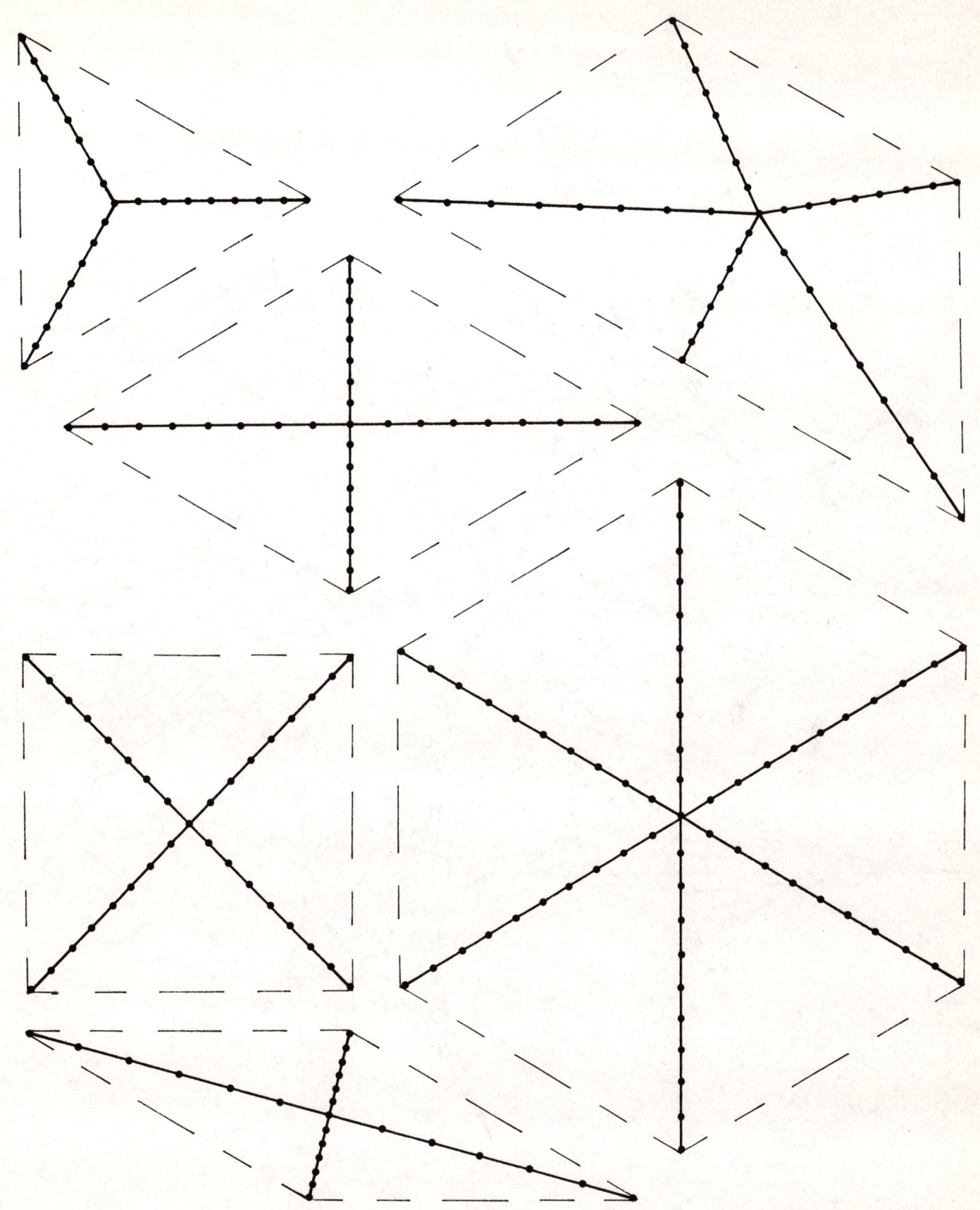

Line Designs

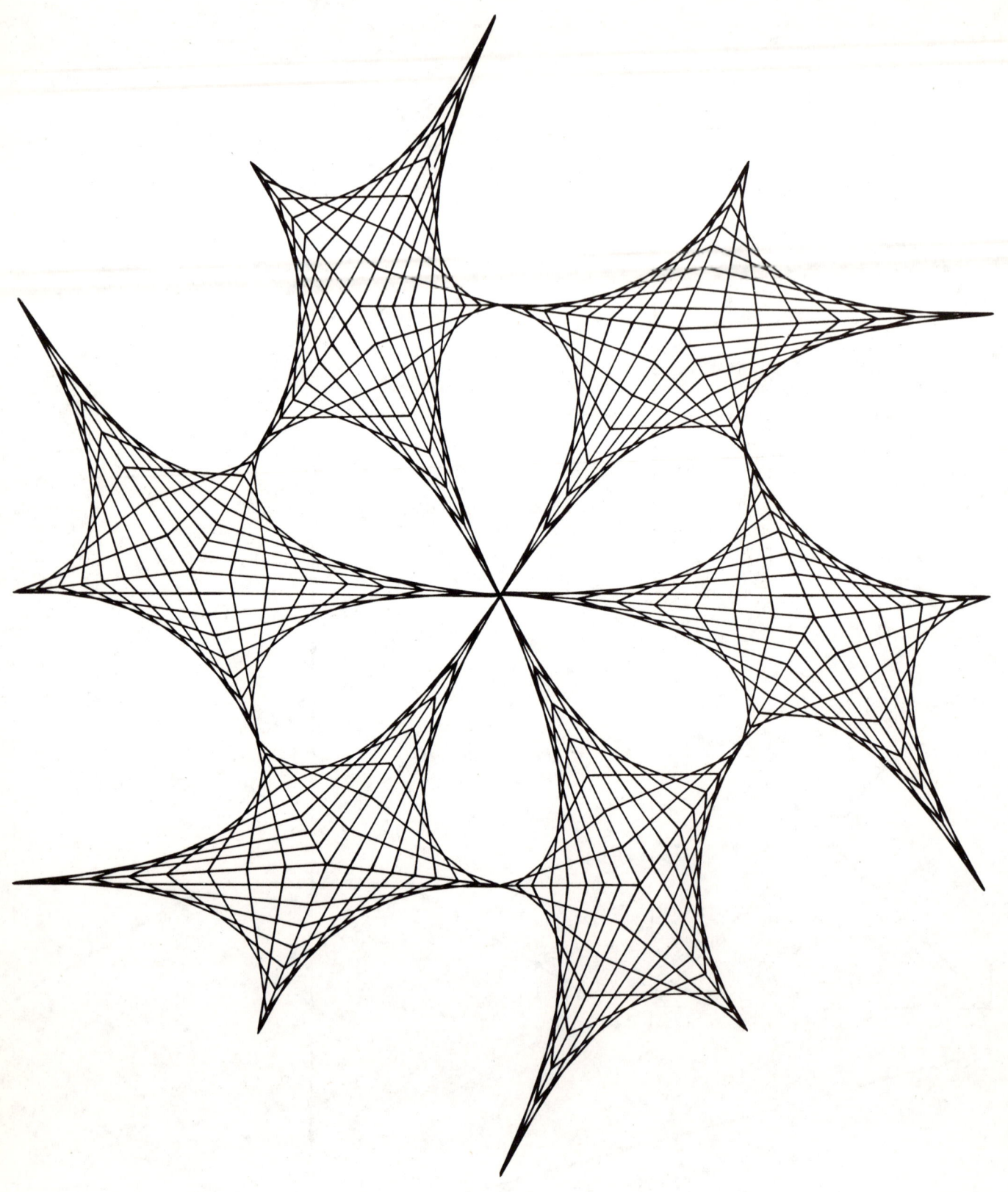

Line Designs

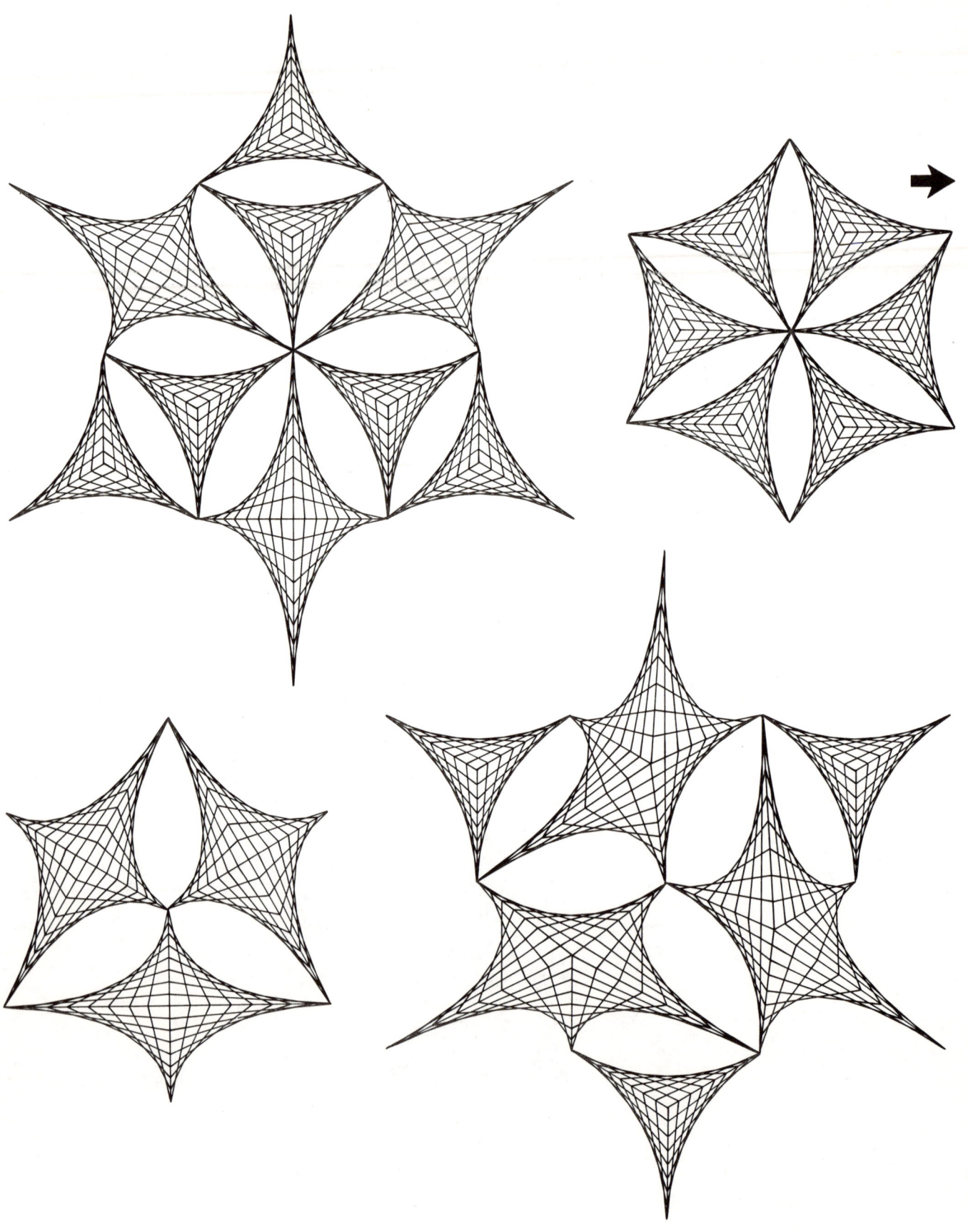

66

©Ideal School Supply Company

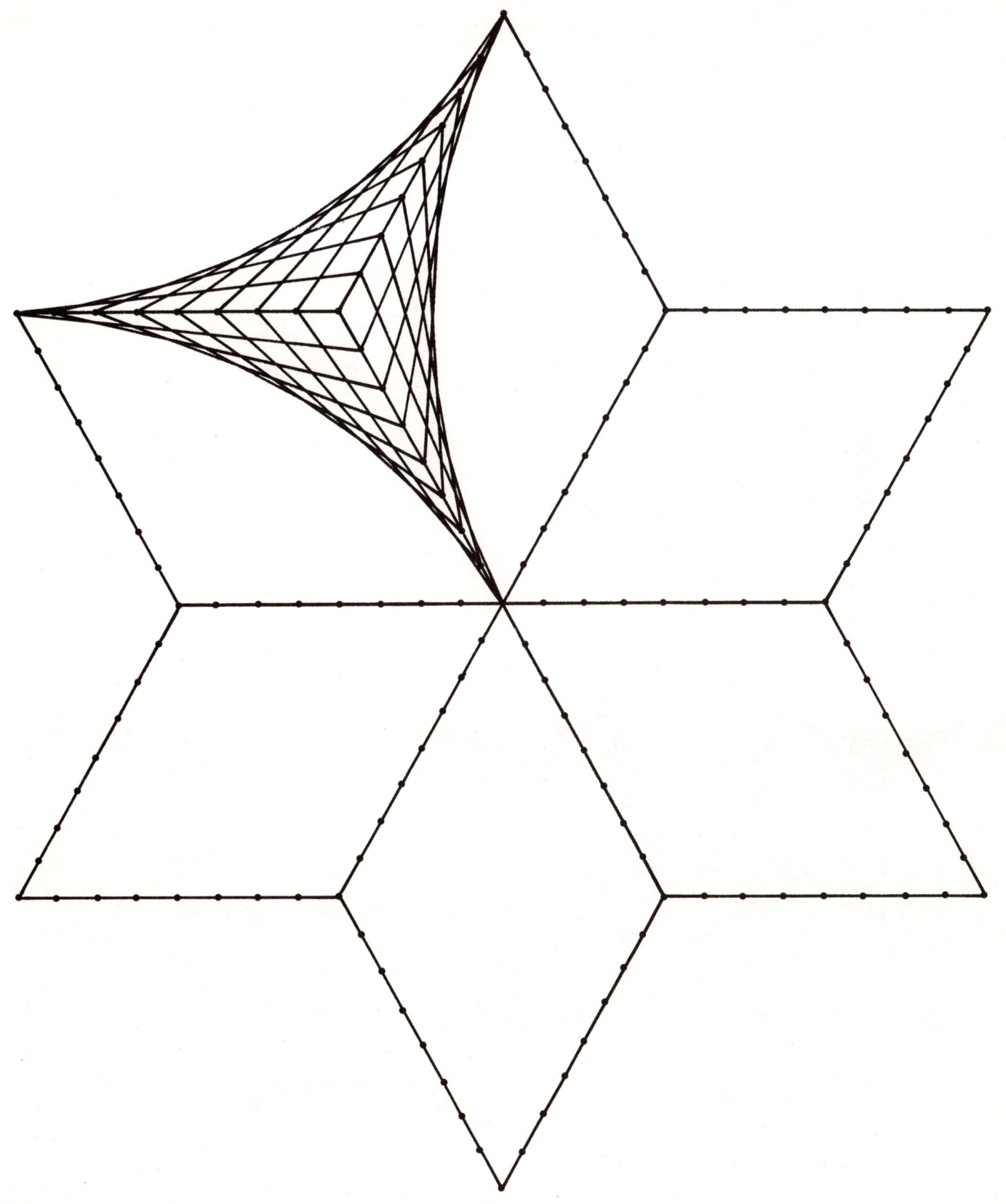

Line Designs

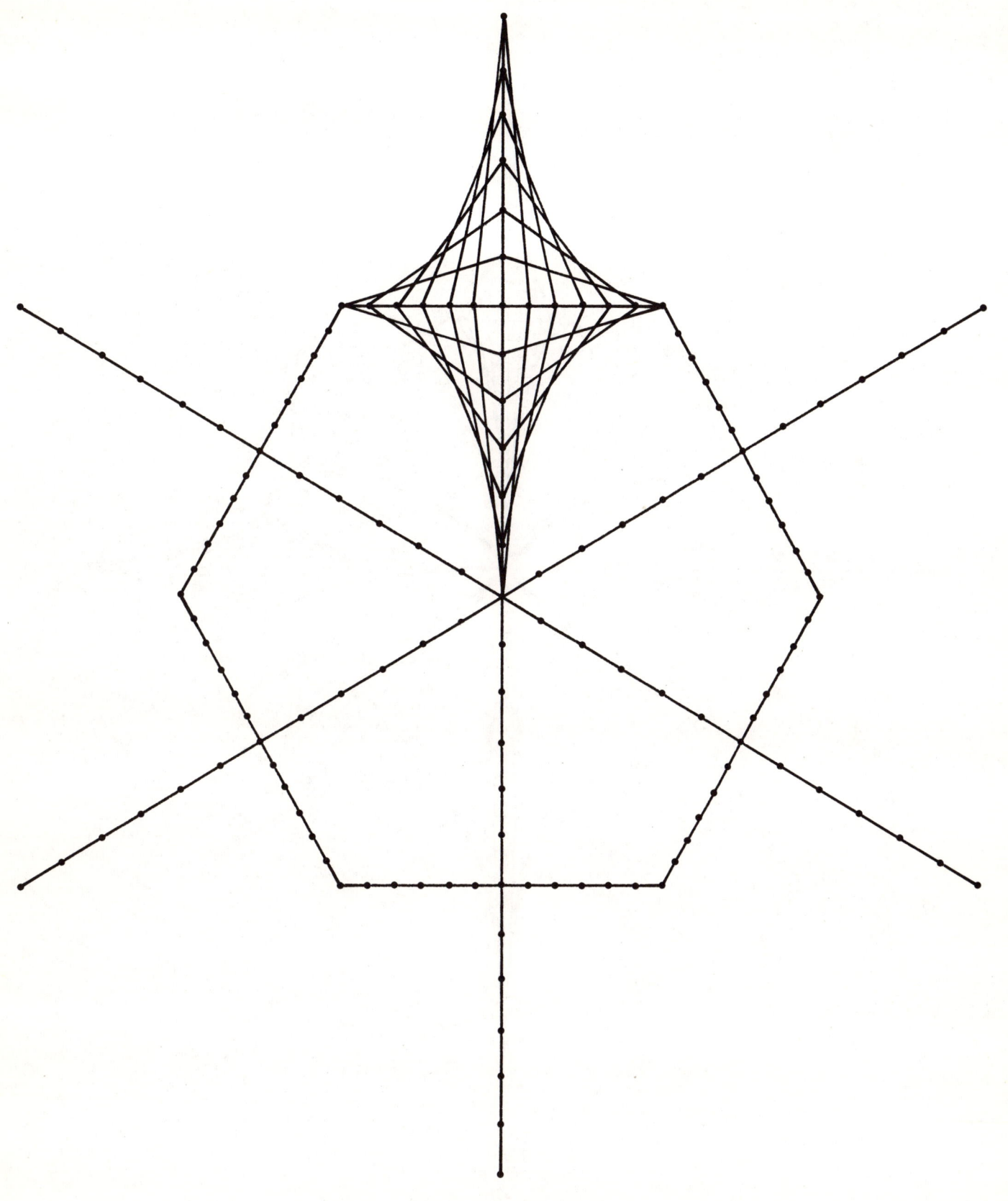

CURVE STITCHING

Beautiful wall hangings can be created by sewing geometric designs on a rigid background with colored thread. This procedure is often called "curve stitching." Once you have learned the technique of drawing line designs, curve stitching is simple. Instead of making a design by drawing a series of line segments connecting two points, the design is made from colored thread, string, or yarn stretched between two points. The materials you will need are a straight edge, pencils, paper, 6 to 14 ply posterboard, tape, scissors, colored thread, a sewing needle, and push pins.

Steps 1 and 2

INSTRUCTIONS

Step 1 — Select a design

Your first design should be a simple one so that you can learn the techniques of curve stitching. It may be a good idea to practice on an angle or two whose sides are divided into eight or ten parts.

Step 2 — Draw the pattern

Draw the basis for the design on a sheet of paper. This is your pattern. It isn't necessary to draw the line design itself on the paper, but you may wish to refer to the complete drawing as you proceed.

Step 3 — Punching the holes

Position the pattern on the cardboard. Hold in position with paper clips or drafting tape. Warning: if you use transparent tape you may ruin the cardboard surface when you remove it. Be sure to center your drawing on the cardboard if it is cut to its final size.

Once the pattern is secured you are ready to punch the holes. Push the push-pins completely through the pattern and cardboard at the points which are the endpoints of the segments of the design. A compass point or needle may be substituted for a push pin. If you use a needle you may need a thimble to protect your thumb.

Step 3a

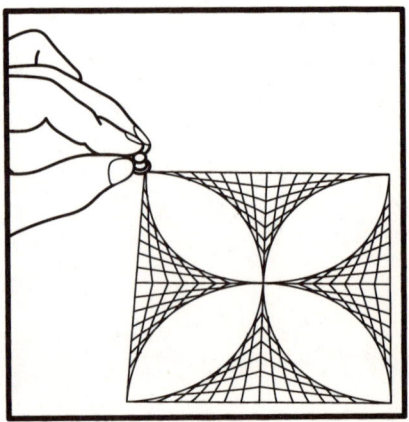

Step 3b

Line Designs

Step 3c

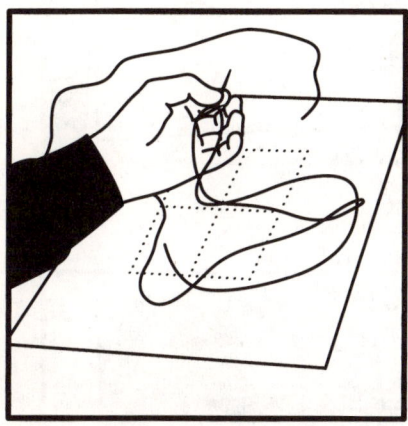
Step 4

Step 5

Step 4 — Threading the needle

Cut a piece of thread two or three meters long. Thread the needle so that about one-third is doubled and two-thirds is single thread. This keeps the needle from becoming unthreaded.

Step 5 — Attaching the thread to cardboard

Tape the end of the thread to the back of the cardboard at a point near the hole where you plan to begin. Don't cover any other holes with the tape.

Step 6 — Stitching and finishing

Push the threaded needle through the beginning hole from the back side. Pull the thread all the way through the hole. Pull it taut to see if your tape is secure. Next find the hole that is the other endpoint of the thread line segment. Push the needle down through that hole and pull the thread all the way through. You should have one "thread segment" on the front of the cardboard. Come back through the next hole in your design pattern and continue this process until the design is finished. When you have used up a length of thread or when you have completed the design, you should finish with the needle and thread on the back of the design. Cut the thread a short distance from the last hole and tape it down securely. You may wish to add extra tape across the other threads on the back for additional security. Trim the posterboard to the desired size and frame or mat your creation.

(see next page for illustrations of Step 6)

Step 6

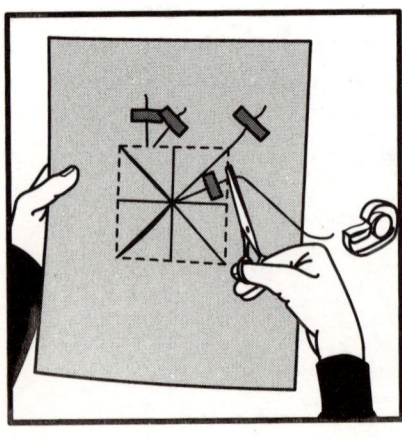
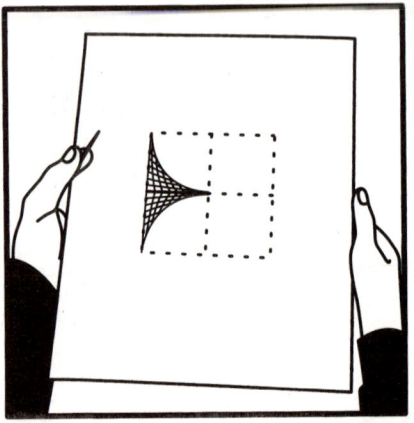

Line Designs
74
©Ideal School Supply Company

CURVE STITCHING VARIATIONS

Several materials and methods can be used to create beautiful curve stitchings. The choice of materials will, of course, depend on the intended display of the final product. Some of the options are discussed below.

Fabric, such as felt, velvet, burlap, canvas, can be stretched over a frame and stitched. After fabric has been stretched tightly over a frame, a staple gun will secure it conveniently. Since it is difficult to draw on fabric it is helpful to tape the pattern to the back of the fabric and leave it there while the design is being stitched. Harder backing such as wood, masonite and plywood can be used if holes are drilled or nails are pounded into the face.

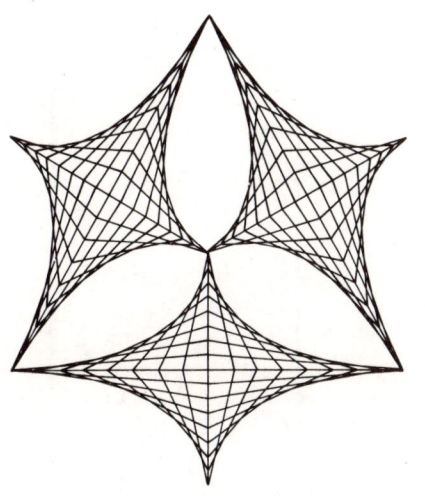

Scratch board, a clay coated material available in black or white at art supply stores, can be used to make attractive designs when the black board is scratched with a sharp pointed instrument, like a needle, pin or compass point, a white line results. If the white board is scratched, a black line appears. Scratch board line designs can be striking, but the material is expensive and requires careful handling.

If harder backings, like masonite and plywood, are used it is necessary to drill sewing holes or pound nails into the face of the board to secure the thread. The line design in Figure 3 was made on a four foot by four foot piece of 1/8 inch masonite. The pattern (see p. 49) was traced onto the board from an overhead projector. The holes were drilled with a 1/4" electric drill, easier and neater than a hand drill, and the design was threaded with colored yarn. If designs are made with nails rather than holes to secure the yarn, it is important to pound all nails to the same depth and to keep them vertical.

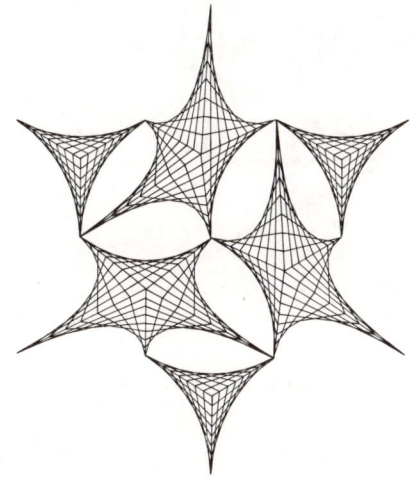

Line Designs

BASIC GEOMETRIC CONSTRUCTIONS

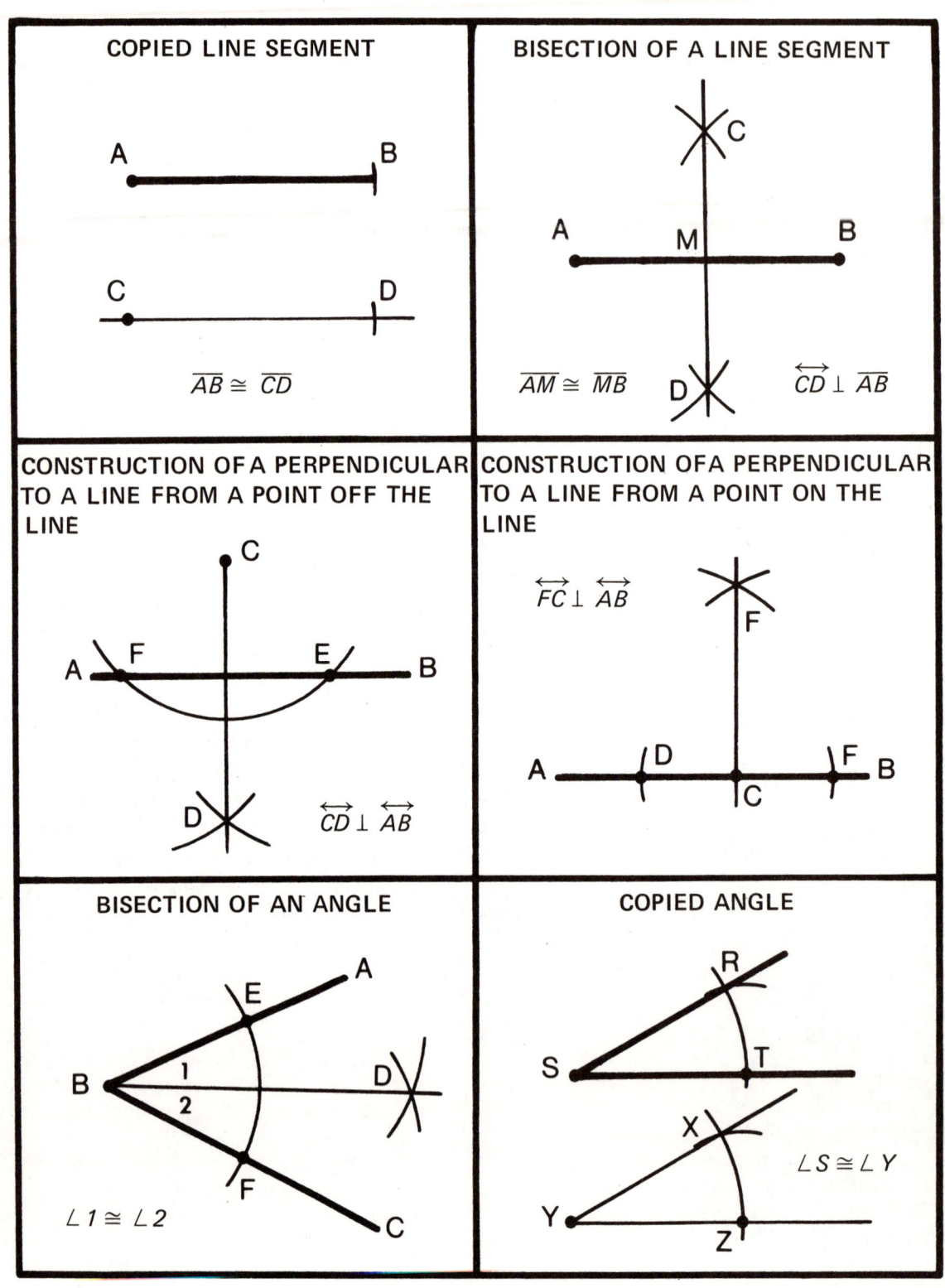

From *Creative Constructions* by Seymour and Schadler ©Ideal School Supply Company

INSCRIBING REGULAR POLYGONS

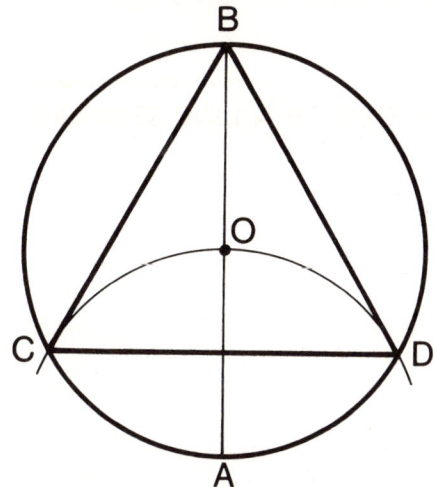

INSCRIBE AN EQUILATERAL TRIANGLE

1. In the given circle O, draw a diameter $\overline{AB}$.
2. Using A as a center and AO as a radius, draw an arc intersecting the circle at C and D.
3. Connect B, C, and D to form the triangle.

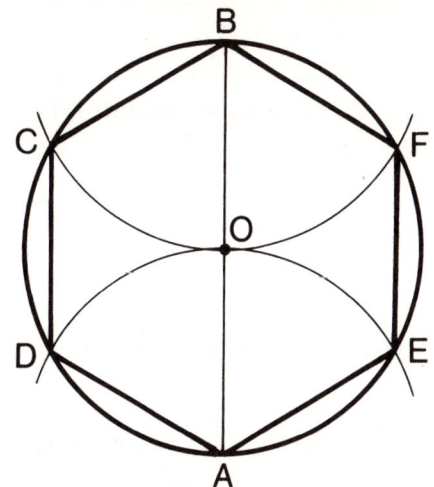

INSCRIBE A REGULAR HEXAGON

1. In the given circle O, draw a diameter $\overline{AB}$.
2. Using A and B as centers and AO as a radius, draw arcs intersecting the circle at C, D, E, and F.
3. Connect A, E, F, B, C, and D to form the hexagon.

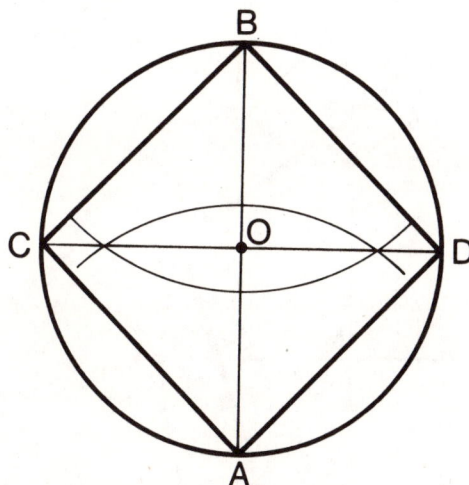

INSCRIBE A SQUARE

1. In the given circle O, draw a diameter $\overline{AB}$.
2. Construct another diameter, $\overline{CD}$, which is the perpendicular bisector of $\overline{AB}$.
3. Connect A, D, B, and C to form the square.

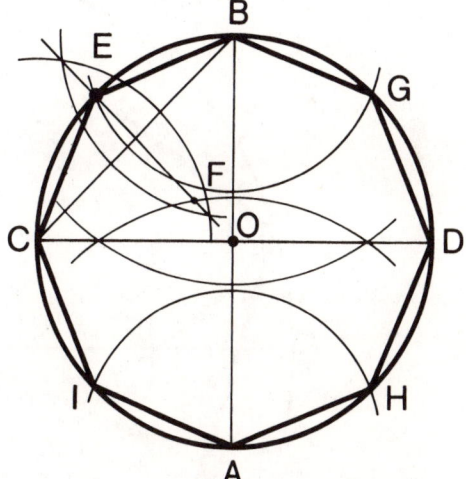

INSCRIBE A REGULAR OCTAGON

1. In the given circle O, locate points A, B, C, and D as in the construction for inscribing a square.
2. Draw $\overline{BC}$ and construct $\overline{EF}$, the perpendicular bisector of $\overline{BC}$.
3. Using A and B as centers and BE as a radius, draw arcs intersecting the circle at G, H, and I.
4. Connect A, I, C, E, B, G, D, and H to form the octagon.

From *Creative Constructions* **by Seymour and Schadler ©Ideal School Supply Company**

INSCRIBING A REGULAR PENTAGON

1. In the given circle, *O*, draw a diameter, *AB*.

2. Construct another diameter, *CD*, which is the perpendicular bisector of *AB*.

3. Bisect *OB*. Label its midpoint *M*.

4. Using *M* as a center and *CM* as a radius, draw an arc intersecting *AO* at *E*.

5. *CE* is the required length of one side of the inscribed regular pentagon.

6. Mark five arcs with radius *CE* on the circle and connect their intersections to form the regular pentagon.

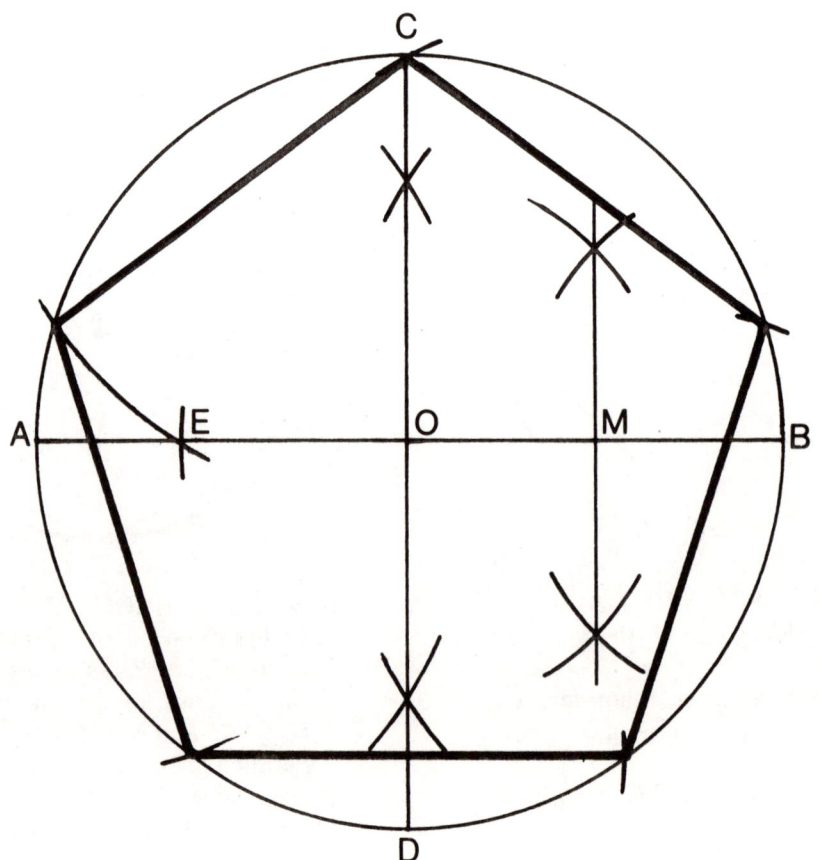

From *Creative Constructions* **by Seymour and Schadler ©Ideal School Supply Company**

Also available from Ideal School Supply Company:

CREATIVE CONSTRUCTIONS, ID10021
by Seymour and Schadler

Creative Constructions is a design and construction book that the authors recommend be used to complement activities from *Line Designs*. The book contains more than 250 designs all constructed with only a straight edge and a compass. Students should be familiar with the basic construction techniques explained in *Creative Constructions* before advancing to the activities in *Line Designs*.

Geometric Design Posters, ID60140

A set of two posters. One poster contains 28 designs from *Line Designs*. The second poster contains 78 figures from *Creative Constructions*.

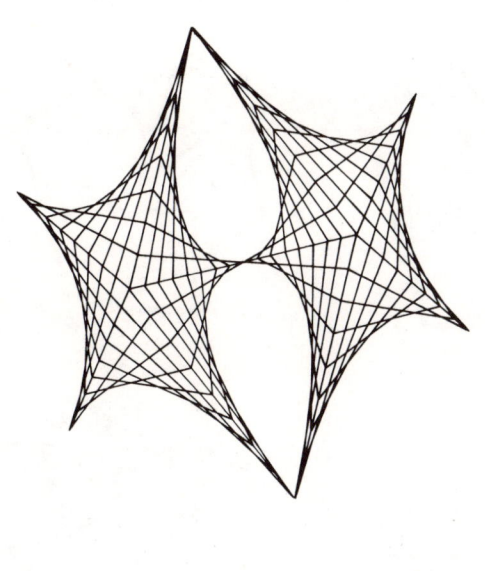
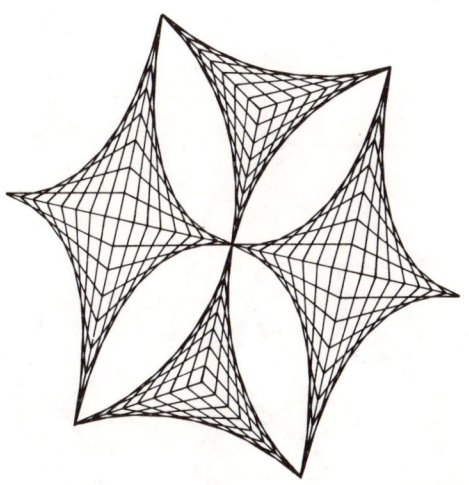

From *Creative Constructions* **by Seymour and Schadler** ©Ideal School Supply Company

From *Creative Constructions* by Seymour and Schadler ©Ideal School Supply Company

Line Designs